The Sunrise Remembers

MERCER
UNIVERSITY PRESS

Endowed by
TOM WATSON BROWN
and
THE WATSON-BROWN FOUNDATION, INC.

The Sunrise Remembers

Memories from the Journey

Jackie K. Cooper

You are the best.

Jackie K. Cooper

Mercer University Press
Macon, Georgia

MUP/P381

© 2008 Mercer University Press
1400 Coleman Avenue
Macon, Georgia 31207
All rights reserved

First Edition.

Books published by Mercer University Press are printed on acid free paper that meets
the requirements of American National Standard for Information Sciences—
Permanence of Paper for Printed Library Materials.

Mercer University Press is a member of Green Press initiative
(greenpressinitiative.org), a nonprofit organization working to help publishers and
printers increase their use of recycled paper and decrease their use of fiber derived
from endangered forests. This book is printed on recycled paper.

Library of Congress Cataloging-in-Publication Data

Cooper, Jackie K.
The sunrise remembers : memories from the journey / Jackie K. Cooper. –
1st ed.
p. cm.
ISBN-13: 978-0-88146-124-4 (pbk. : alk. paper)
ISBN-10: 0-88146-124-5 (pbk. : alk. paper)
1. Cooper, Jackie K.—Anecdotes. 2. Critics—Georgia—Anecdotes.
3.Journalists—Georgia—Anecdotes. 4. Early memories—Georgia. 5.Sun—
Rising and setting. 6. Georgia—Biography—Anecdotes. 7. South Carolina—
Biography—Anecdotes. I. Title.
CT275.C775142A3 2008
9758'515092—dc22
[B]
2008030494

For Natalie

The Newest Resident of my Heart

Contents

Acknowledgments

With each book I write, the list of people I should thank grows longer and longer. It would be impossible for me to list all of the members of my family, my fellow writers, my friends, and my most loyal readers who support me in every way. I must simply say you know who you are and are loved and appreciated by me.

I do want to single out Marc Jolley and his staff at Mercer University Press. We've done it again, guys. Who would have known we would have five books under our belt! It's a miracle.

And finally once again my thanks to my mother Virginia who told me I was special and to my wife Terry who helps me believe it.

Foreword

In early 2006, Jackie Cooper mentioned to me that his publisher, Mercer University Press, had asked him if I'd be interested in writing a blurb for the jacket of his new book *The Bookbinder*. I was flattered. Jackie and I had been friends for more than six years, and, through my work with Georgia Public Broadcasting, I had become very familiar with both the man and his writing.

I read the page proofs the Press sent me and set about crafting my blurb, mindful of the great authors and critics throughout time who have been asked to add their imprimatur to some new tome and who have presumably struggled to find the right balance between profundity and promotion. Here's what I came up with: "There is a wise man in Georgia by the name of Jackie K. Cooper. His wisdom stems from his fervent humanity, which is emblazoned across every page of *The Bookbinder*. Set forth in these pages are the simple things that make us human and bind us together as we weep or as we laugh, as we regret or as we rejoice. Jackie K. Cooper is indeed the bookbinder, and he has learned his trade well."

Obviously I did something right because now I've now been asked to write the foreword to Jackie's most recent book, *The Sunrise Remembers: Memories from the Journey*, and as I reread what I wrote about *The Bookbinder* I realize that not much has changed; what I said back then still holds true for this new book. Jackie's "fervent humanity" is "emblazoned across every page" of *The Sunrise Remembers* as well, and he is still "a wise man."

This wisdom he possesses is the wisdom of the poet, that intangible knowledge, lesson, or reflection that is given linguistic form and rhetorical life by the person with that special poetic gift.

Jackie is indeed a poet; he not only makes his living fitting different rhetorical devices together in books and reviews, he also embodies his very enterprise. If you were to look up Jackie K. Cooper in a dictionary of rhetorical terms, you'd find his picture under "oxymoron."

One of the things I have always found most endearing about our "poet" is how ordinary he is. He has led an admittedly interesting life, and yet it has been a very ordinary life. I mean no slight in saying this; in fact I think Jackie would be the first to agree with me. His stories celebrate his ordinariness, even those he tells about the famous people he has met over the years. He is always at pains to point out how down to earth and real these celebrities are, and how remarkable that he, little old Jackie K. Cooper, can get to talk to them. His stories talk of the ordinary things of life: family, death, illness, weddings, holidays, memories etc. These are commonplaces of our existence, and Jackie revels in them. I wonder if his favorite movie is *Ordinary People*?

So what makes him an oxymoron? Well, he might be the poster child for "ordinary," but I find him to be completely extraordinary. His ability to take the most mundane aspects of his life, as recorded in his journals, and craft them into stories that have such power and universality is extraordinary. And if you doubt this power, read Jackie's introduction to *The Bookbinder* where he explains how he came by the book's title:

A few years ago I was selling books at the Cherry Blossom Festival in Macon, Georgia. A lady came into the booth and told me she had read all of my books. She then asked me if I knew what she called them. I couldn't imagine what word she would use, but several negative choices raced through my mind. Still I managed to ask her what she did call them, and she answered "my comfort books." It seems she read a story whenever she had had a bad day, or when she just needed a pick me up. She then added "You write stories that bind us together."

I was so flattered by that statement, and I thought about it long and hard when I got home. I realized I had reached my goal, as I had always wanted my stories to be a means to bind people together or to make them relate to events I described. I also decided at that moment that my next book would be titled *The Bookbinder*. Hopefully it too would be a gathering of stories that would bind people together through shared memories.

Jackie knows the power, the universality that his stories can have. There is indeed something extraordinary in this ordinary man's life.

Several years ago I was invited to give a commencement address at Georgia Southern University. I knew I had to give some sort of inspirational speech, something that would wave the new graduates off out into the big wide world and on to bigger and better achievements.

The only thing I could really draw on for my remarks was my close involvement with books and authors. These have been the basis of my professional career for a couple of decades and so I considered literature the best bet for presenting meaningful and authoritative comments to those about to begin new chapters in their lives.

Focusing on the theme of the importance of the path one takes in life, I spoke of the opening lines of Dante's *Divine Comedy* in which he awakes to find himself in a dark wood and realizes he has strayed from the "straight path." One helluva (pun intended) journey later, Dante has been set back on the straight and narrow, thanks in no small part to his guide, the Roman poet Virgil.

I went on to cite the much more widely read poem by Robert Frost, "The Road Not Taken," because it echoes so much of what Dante was talking about.

> Two roads diverged in a yellow wood,
> And sorry I could not travel both
> And be one traveler, long I stood
> And looked down one as far as I could
> To where it bent in the undergrowth;
> Then took the other, as just as fair,
> And having perhaps the better claim,
> Because it was grassy and wanted wear;

We're back almost in Dante's dark wood again. Frost's poetic "I" has before him two roads and, after much thought, elects to take, not the road he's been scrutinizing, but the other because, as he says, "it was grassy and wanted wear." It is the road less traveled; the road whose way has not been worn down by previous travelers. He chooses then the more difficult road, not knowing what lies ahead. He rejects the easy way, just as Dante is forced to resume his life's journey on the straight road, the road to Heaven, not the easy road that leads to Hell.

So where does Jackie Cooper come into this? Well, as I developed my commencement theme, I realized that it was my old friend Jackie who could tie Dante and Frost together and help me make my point: the road you take in life makes all the difference; following your heart makes all the difference. As Frost concludes, "I took the one [road] less traveled by/ And that has made all the difference." You may have to take the road less traveled, but it *will* make all the difference.

In the Prologue to his second book, *Chances and Choices*, Jackie writes, "In life everything is one of two things—chances or choices. There are those things we choose to do and there are those things that seem to happen to us at random.... We are set off down a road that has many pitfalls and brambles to make our way through. Or just when we think we can't plod through the muck and mire another moment the sun comes out and dries the road and makes it passable once more." There's Jackie sounding a lot like Dante and Frost. He was the perfect person to tie the whole address together and bring it home to Georgia.

So my three chosen poets for the commencement address were Dante Alighieri (with assistance from Publius Virgilius Naso), Robert Frost, and Jackie K. Cooper.

But can Cooper really be considered a poet? Well yes, certainly. A prose poet maybe, but certainly no less lyrical. His writing has a power beyond its sphere in the same way that of Dante's or Frost's does.

Consider this passage from W. R. Johnson's *The Idea of Lyric: Lyric Modes in Ancient and Modern Poetry*:

> The task of the lyric poet is neither to report accurately, in the false sense of mimesis [imitation, representation], an actual event and the emotions it gave rise to (which is not really possible, in any case, as anyone who has tried and failed to do this knows); nor is his task to invent emotions that he has never experienced (which is neither really possible nor, so limitless the supply of experience for poet and nonpoet alike, necessary). What distinguishes the lyric poet from people who are not lyric poets is perhaps, in part, his extreme sensitivity to

emotions; but more important here is his ability to arrange his perceptions of emotion into clear patterns by means of precise language. In shaping emotions, then, the lyric poet performs two very different, indeed, opposite, functions simultaneously; he particularizes a universal emotion or cluster of emotions, such as all men share—that is to say, he dramatizes the universal, makes it vivid and plausible; and, at the same time, he universalizes an experience that is or was peculiarly his own, thus rendering it clear and intelligible. It is this delicate yet powerful fusion of the individual and the universal that characterizes good lyric poetry. (32–33)

Here we have exactly what Jackie does in his stories. He is in touch with his feelings; he is able to get things down on paper clearly; and, the genius of it all, he dramatizes the universal and universalizes an experience that was initially his own. What he tells us of his life speaks to us all. He does, as his fan put it, "bind us together." He is the poet supreme!

As slight as Jackie's stories may appear, don't be fooled by their brevity. These stories from his journey have a power beyond our ken. Such is the skill of the true poet.

And don't be fooled by what may seem like the time-bound nature of his experiences. Jackie is still the master of his trade and so time has no role to play here because, as our poet reminds us with appropriate rhetorical flourish, "the sunrise remembers."

St.John Flynn
Director of Cultural Programming
KUHF Houston Public Radio
Former Host, *Cover to Cover*
Georgia Public Broadcasting Radio

Prologue

It took me a while, but I finally realized memories are the stories of our lives. What you recall each day in your memory are the stories that have happened to you in the past. Remember that old song by Dean Martin called "Memories Are Made of This"? Well old Dino was right. Each day we are living tomorrow's memories.

When I was a little boy I didn't know about memories as such. I was just having the fun of the experience of living. It took a summer day and a wise woman to let me know that my life was about making memories.

I must have been around six years old when my mother and father decided to open a corner grocery store. The lot our house sat on was actually a double lot and so there was room on the corner for a small concrete block building to be erected. It became Cooper's Grocery.

The "store" as we called it was a place where you could buy canned goods, cold drinks, and kerosene (There was a pump out back.). My mother ran the store and my daddy kept his job with the Merita Bread Company as a salesman. We always had plenty of bread and cakes to eat.

After the store opened it became a gathering place of sorts for people in the neighborhood. Two of my favorite people were Aunt Ida and Aunt Lula. Aunt Ida was a tall raw-boned woman of an indeterminate age. Aunt Lula was small to begin with and age had slumped her over. Still she was feisty and fun.

Aunt Ida was the talker of the two. She would sit outside on a bench and tell me story after story about our neighborhood and the town in general. She knew everything or at least so it seemed to my six-year-old mind. I never tired of listening to her and would beg for another story when the last one ended.

One day I asked her just how she knew so much. It amazed me how she could collect such a large amount of knowledge. When she answered me I was totally shocked. She told me in the clearest of terms that when she put her head on her pillow each night every thought went away. She said her head was as empty during the night as could be.

I argued with her that she couldn't be telling the truth. If all her thoughts left each night, how could she know so much the next day? "Honey child," she said, "the sunrise remembers. And as long as that sun comes up each day, the memories you have created will always come back. That's the way the good Lord meant it to be and that is the way it is."

That answer satisfied me, and since I never thought to wake up in the middle of the night and test it I believed it for quite some time. I slept the sleep of the innocent and the sunrise brought me back my memories each morning.

Years later when my mother was dying of cancer I panicked at the thought I might forget some of the wonderful times we had had. I was afraid I would forget her touch and the way she looked. This fear of forgetting was enough to cause me to be afraid of the future. But then it came to me. Aunt Ida's voice sounded in my head and told me that as long as the sunrise remembered I could never forget.

A lot of years have passed since that time and numerous sunrises have come and gone. Each day still brings me my memories and some of them make up the stories in this book. My memories link me to the past, but they also prepare me for the future. I have gone back to the years 2002 and 2003 for these stories. This was a time when both of my grandchildren had been born and I was settling into retirement (of a sort).

Cherish the memories you have. Hopefully mine will trigger some of yours. They are there inside you and wait every night for the sunrise to remember.

Reflections from Route 2002

The Ties that Bind

From the day I was born I was extremely close to my mother. I don't know if somewhere inside me I knew I would lose her at an early age, but something told me our time together was precious. I was content to spend most of my time with her and I had to know where she was at all times.

I remember hearing a friend of hers say that she had never seen a child as attached to his mother as I was to her. She said there seemed to be some invisible cord that stretched between the two of us. And it was true. I knew when she would step outside the house, I could actually feel her absence. Later when I went to school I would start calling her name as soon as I got within earshot of the house. If she was not at home I would concentrate and somehow I would know which of the neighbor's houses she was visiting. Off I would go and listen to her talk with her friends.

Now this doesn't mean I didn't have friends. I did. And I played with them for hours at a time, but there was always that special time I spent with my mother. The time that was making memories that I would have for a lifetime.

When my mother died I felt our cord had been severed. I was adrift in a stormy sea and I just knew I would never find solid footing without her. For those first few days after she died I was in a state of semi-consciousness. I moved like a zombie or a sleepwalker.

Gradually I began to awaken and realized just what my life had become, and I was not happy. The future appeared to be totally bleak to me and I saw no hope for happiness. But then I began to feel a tug towards who she was and what she had been.

The cord that had been slack between us began to tighten once more.

As I moved through my teenage years I was faced with decisions to make as to how I wanted to live my life. At each fork in the road I could feel a tug and I know that she led me in the right path. That isn't to say I didn't make some wrong decisions, but overall I think I made mostly right ones.

Eventually I became an adult and I was completely responsible for myself. The cord became loose again and I moved about with only my own conscience to guide me. I had become the person she wanted me to be.

Today there are new invisible cords between me and my wife, my two sons, and my grandchildren. I feel the connections. They aren't as strong as that original one was, but they are still there. They tug at my heart from time to time and that is a good feeling.

The tie between a parent and a child is strong, or can be. I was lucky because the tie between my mother and me was unbreakable. It bound us together for a lifetime.

A Wedding Reminder

This past week my wife and I went to a wedding. It was one of the few we have been to this summer. Usually we are swamped by these events, but either we were out of town when the other weddings occurred or we didn't feel a real need to attend. This one was the marriage of the son of some good friends of ours so we were eager to go.

Weddings to me are always pretty and nice. The bride always looks beautiful, and the couple always looks happy. But what I enjoy most of all is that this is a time when we get to see a lot of our good friends. Since we moved to Perry all those millions of years ago, we have been blessed to have great friends. And we all know each other so well that most of our best friends are best friends.

When I was growing up in South Carolina I went from kindergarten through college with the same group of close friends. Our parents all knew each other and we went to the same schools. These were good friends of mine and I always thought I would never find people I could be as close to as I was to them.

I still have some of those friends. We stay in touch but only sporadically. They have new lives, new spouses, new children, and new jobs. When we do get together, it is to talk of the past. That is what we have in common.

My two best friends, Chuck and Hollis, have stayed part of my life but mostly through memories. Chuck died a few years ago, and I haven't talked with Hollis in over a year. But when I get nostalgic I go back in my mind to those days when the three of us were inseparable. We were not alike in most ways. Hollis was a great athlete while Chuck played sports but wasn't too good. I was a total washout at any game.

Then there was popularity. I sought it out. Hollis took it as his due. Chuck lived on the borders of the "in" group. But one thing we had in common. We were all pretty smart. I made the best grades because I studied the hardest. Hollis coasted along, his mind more on basketball than books. Chuck was a genius but never applied himself. He had a mind that was scary. All of that science stuff that drove me crazy, he sailed through with little effort.

Some of my best memories are of sitting up all night with those guys to solve the problems of the world. We just knew if we were in charge we could get it done. But somehow we never did put that problem solving into action. Chuck became a research chemist. Hollis taught school and coached basketball. And I went off to law school and tried to be a lawyer. It didn't take even though I gave it ten years or so.

Still, being a lawyer is what brought me to middle Georgia. I came here to work as a civilian attorney at Robins Air Force Base. My wife and I decided to move to Perry and that is where we started making our friends. It happened quickly that the people we love became our friends early on. We were like loose magnets that were drawn to each other.

So, as I sat at that wedding, I looked around and saw that most of us had gathered there, and them being around me gave me a feeling of completeness. I thought about a song that says, "Most friends are made through smiles and tears, and some friendships fade over miles and years." My Perry friendships haven't faded. Even the friends who have moved away from Perry are still close to us. I think it is the magic of Perry that makes friendships deeper and eternally lasting.

The Changes Keep on Coming

For someone who doesn't like change, the changes keep on coming. First off my son and daughter-in-law are moving into a new house. I can handle that one. But it is hard on my granddaughter Genna. She is only two and a half years old but she already doesn't like change —at all. It is the Cooper curse.

My wife Terry and I went to Moultrie to help Sean move some things into the new place while Genna, her brother Walker, and her mother were all visiting in Hawkinsville. After we got Genna's room all fixed up, Sean asked what we thought. Terry and I both agreed it was a perfect little girl's room. But his concern really was what did we think Genna would think of it.

"You know how she is about change," he said. "We haven't even told her we're moving. It just upsets her. She wants everything to stay the same."

I nodded my head knowing exactly how she feels. But I also know she will get through it. Just like I will. Change is inevitable.

Two years ago my oldest son J.J. moved to Macon from Tennessee. He had decided life was too short to be that far away from family. His grandfather had just died and I think that made him miss home and family more than ever. Plus he is crazy about his niece and now his new nephew.

But a month or so ago he told me he had applied for a job with *Baseball America*. This is a baseball newspaper/ magazine that is printed every two weeks. The position, which was open, was that of an editor. After a couple of weeks I asked if he had heard anything from them. He answered no and said he didn't think they were interested in him.

Now, I know I think my kids walk on water, but honestly, how could a sports publication not be interested in him? He lives, breathes, and eats sports. And he is good at writing and editing. Strike that—he is great at writing and editing! I couldn't understand their lack of interest.

A few days later he called and said the magazine had contacted him. The guy who would do the interviews had been on vacation. They now wanted J.J. to fly to their home office in Durham, North Carolina, for an interview. I could see the writing on the wall.

To make a long story short, he was offered the job. I knew he would be. When he asked me what I thought, I couldn't believe the answer I gave. "Of course you have to take it," I said. "It is the opportunity of a lifetime for you. It would be like me being asked to write for *Variety* or the *Hollywood Reporter*. It's what you've always wanted."

Inside I was dying. What I wanted to do was beg him not to take it. But sometimes we rise to the occasion and say what is best for our child and not what is best for us. J.J. took the job. He leaves in four weeks.

I don't like change. I fight against change. But for my children, their happiness comes first. On my scales of life, happiness for them far outweighs my need to keep everything the same. So I will send him off with a smile on my face and a lump in my throat.

And before he is out of that driveway I will be planning the trip Terry and I will be making to Durham. It's only a seven-hour drive.

My Big Fat Protestant Wedding

The new movie *My Big Fat Greek Wedding* is playing in Macon. I urge you to go to see it. It is as funny a film as you will see any other time this year. What is even more amazing is that it is both funny and relatively clean—a real rarity these days.

The story concerns a young Greek woman living in the United States. She wants to be like everyone else but her huge extended Greek family wants to keep alive all the old traditions. When she meets the love of her life, a non-Greek guy, she is afraid the collective family she is attached to will drive him away.

The amazing thing about the movie is that anyone and everyone can relate to it. There are enough aunts, uncles, and cousins on screen that you are bound to find one or two that reminds you of someone in your family. I know I found a few of mine hiding in there.

My mother's family was always more interesting than my father's. They were just a tad more eccentric. The star of the show was my Aunt Myrna. She always thought she was a little bit better than the rest of the family. She and her family lived in Clinton just as we did, but Aunt Myrna and her family had lived there longer so therefore the town belonged to her.

All of us belonged to the First Baptist Church so we all gathered there each and every Sunday. Aunt Myrna sang in the choir and she stood in the very middle of the very front row where she could be seen and admired by all. I don't know how old I was when it dawned on me that Aunt Myrna looked different when she was in the choir. She seemed to stand out from the others.

When I asked my mother she replied it was because Aunt Myrna looked like death warmed over. I didn't understand that so I asked for more of an explanation. My mother then explained that Myrna powdered her face a deathly white before she went into church each Sunday. She thought skin that was tanned to the slightest degree was trashy, so she opted for the Morticia Addams look and went with pale.

My Aunt Agnes was also a member of the same church. She was on Daddy's side of the family by marriage. Aunt Agnes thought she was pretty high falutin' too, but she would speak to you. And when she spoke she trilled. That's the only way I know to describe it. She just gave all of her conversation a little song and trill effect. Most of the time it was off key but, that was her way of talking. Maybe she saw life as a musical and she was the star. Who knows?

Then there was Uncle Derek, mother's brother in law. Rumor had it that Uncle Derek had been a member of the Klan in his early life in Alabama. My cousin Sara swore that she was over at his and Aunt Pat's house one day and saw the sheet with the holes for eyes and all.

My mother of course denied all of this. She was horrified to even think of such a thing, but all of us cousins thought it was true and we steered clear of Uncle Derek.

Every family has its oddballs and quirky members. You aren't a true Southerner if you don't have one or two. And according to this movie families all over have them. So go see *My Big Fat Greek Wedding*. It might make you nostalgic for some of your old relatives you haven't seen in a while.

Retired? You Bet.

It amazes me every day to think that I am retired. In a lot of ways I am living out the American Dream. Honestly, though, I never thought much about retirement when I was living my career as a federal employee. It was always something in the future that wasn't near at hand. I didn't talk about retirement; I didn't think about retirement; I didn't really plan for retirement. It just happened.

One day I was working and the next I was at home. I had taken some time off and really planned to go back to work. But as the time neared I checked my eligibility and saw I met all the requirements for retirement, so I stayed home. This really fit in with my plans as I didn't want a farewell luncheon, any testimonials, or any gifts. Like General MacArthur, I just wanted to fade away.

It also helped that I only retired from my full-time job. I had already written a couple of books, so I had some commitments to help market them. I also was employed by a TV station as the entertainment critic and I stayed on there. There were still newspaper columns to write and movies to review, so I stayed active.

At the time of this writing, I have my two books to plug; I am still on television each Friday night; I am on the radio four times each weekend; I write a column for the Perry newspaper and also am entertainment critic for them; and I speak to different groups about twice each month, so I stay busy.

Still it is being busy at something I want to do. I don't have to do things I don't want to do, and as a general rule I don't. I could sleep late if I wanted to, but generally I am up by seven. I could travel if I wanted to, but generally I prefer to stay in Georgia or visit only states nearby. I don't have any burning desire to see Europe or Asia, Africa, or Australia. That would mean flying and I still don't like flying at all.

Do you know what I do miss? I miss having holidays and weekends. Okay, I know those events still occur, but they aren't special times like they were when I was a full-time employee. There is a feeling of joy in being a full-time worker and having a holiday or vacation time. You just feel like it is special. As a retiree every day has the potential of being a holiday, a vacation, or a weekend.

Would I go back to work full time just to have the thrill of having a day off? I don't think so. Being free to be what you want to be where you want to be beats that element of joy that comes when you have a day off.

Of course I am constantly amazed that I can sit at home and a paycheck still arrives each and every month. Is this a great country or what?

So come on into the retirement pool, the water's fine. It doesn't mean your life is over, not by a long shot, but you do get a chance to do more of the things you always wanted to do but couldn't because you had to earn a living. There may not be the excitement of getting a day off from work, but having every day off is a giant trade off for that euphoria. I like retirement, and I think you will too.

One Year Later

This week saw the anniversary of the attack on the World Trade Center Towers. It has been a year since those horrible images of destruction flickered across our TV screens. I can well remember how I saw it all, and I am sure you recall where you were and what you thought at the time, too.

When I saw the image of the first plane hitting the tower, I thought it was a terrible, tragic accident. I assumed it was a plane that had been coming in for a landing at one of New York's airports. I thought it had somehow gotten off its path and hit the building. It never dawned on me that it had been driven into the building intentionally.

Then as I watched the television set the second plane flew into the other tower. My mind then asked itself how a tragic accident like this could happen twice. I know that sounds stupid today in light of all that happened, but on September 11, 2001, I couldn't bring my mind to think that people could be so deranged and evil that they would fly two planes full of passengers into those buildings.

Even at my age I still had a sense of innocence about our country, and about people in general. I had never seen a horror like this one. Of course I had read the newspapers and had heard about terrorist attacks in different places around the globe, but I didn't dream it could happen within our borders. But it did, and for a whole country innocence and trust died that day to a large degree.

It has been a year since the attacks. It has been a year full of war and threats and fear. There has been the war against

Afghanistan and the threat of war against Iraq. There have been increased security checks at airports and the installation of sky marshals on certain flights. No longer do we just have the fear of flying; now we have to fear hijacking and attacks in the air.

In May of last year I went to Hawaii. While I was there I went to the Pearl Harbor Memorial where the *USS Arizona* was sunk during the December 7, 1941 attack. I was overcome by the emotion that I felt for those who lost their lives there. I had no idea that another attack on America would be coming so soon.

Some day I will go to New York City and I will visit the site where the twin towers stood. And once again I will be overwhelmed by the loss that occurred there. And I will pray that another such attack never comes.

I pray that my children and my grandchildren can one day have the sense of security and safety that I had always felt up to September 11, 2001. People should be able to trust their fellow men and to think that good will prevail in all instances. I pray that an age of innocence will return some day, but inside I worry that it won't.

Inside, I worry that it can't.

Crazy Families

Unique members of the family. We all have them. At least I know I do. Over the years it has dawned on me that not everyone in the world acts like some of the crazier members of my family do. For example, my unique brother. Every year for my birthday he calls me. Yep, that's my present—a telephone call. Not a tie, a CD or a book—just a long distance telephone call.

Back a few years ago we rarely talked except on my birthday when he called, but recently we have been talking just about every day. I paid extra and got this long distance service on my cell phone that allows me to speak with anyone in Georgia, Florida, Alabama, or South Carolina for free as long as I don't go over my allotted number of minutes. And since my brother, who lives in Florida, has been sick and had surgery, etc., I try to call him at least every other day or so.

Seriously, we do talk on the phone a lot. And we talk at length while he gives me the rundown on his latest ailments. So naturally I expected him to maybe come up with a better gift than the phone call for my birthday this year, especially since I had called him on September 12 and my birthday is on September 13.

On the night of my birthday, promptly at eleven o'clock, the phone rang. I think the long distance rates go down after eleven at night. Anyway, I answered the phone. "Happy birthday," a familiar voice announced. "This is your special birthday call."

"What makes it a special birthday call?" I asked with sarcasm filling every syllable.

"Because I am paying for it," he replied, just as logical as could be.

In his mind that really does make it special. It doesn't matter that I have called him a hundred times in the last few months; on this night he was paying. So happy birthday to me!

Oh, yes, and a few days later he sent me a birthday card. It was one of those cards you send over the Internet. It had a picture of a cat and had a printed message of "Happy Birthday!" The cat looked familiar and soon I knew why. As I gazed at my birthday card the picture changed to an advertisement for *Stuart Little 2*. The cat was "Snowbell" from the movie.

What I can't figure out is why he was sending me a card three days after my birthday and why it was one that featured an advertisement for a movie that came out in July. I am sure there is some logic in there somewhere, but then again maybe not. Maybe that just goes along with being a little nutty, which he has and always will be.

But you know there is something to be said for being consistent. It is reassuring to know that some traditions are still alive and well and that no matter how old I get or how ancient he gets (he is almost four years older than I), the phone call on the birthday is still coming through. In that respect I will opt for crazy relatives every time. Sometimes consistency is a way of showing you are still loved.

My South Carolina Home

For the past thirty-plus years, I have lived in Georgia, but I spent the first twenty-plus years of my life living in South Carolina. And for some reason, being born there will always make me think of South Carolina as home. Even now, after being married and having two children and two grandchildren in middle Georgia, that small house on Holland Street in Clinton, South Carolina, is where my mind automatically goes when someone mentions "home."

I think back some times about how decidedly middle class we were. My daddy was a bread salesman and my mother ran a grocery store. We didn't have a car for the longest time when I was growing up and we were the last people on our street to get a TV. Neither of my parents had a college education and none of their friends did either.

We ate out one day a week and that was on Sunday. We would go to Louie's Restaurant and I would get a hot roast pork sandwich every single week. I was a picky eater but I was a consistent one. My brother got a variety of foods, but no food on his plate could touch the other foods, so he had his idiosyncrasies, too.

My mother and father argued about money constantly. There was never enough. That was the main problem. But my mother spent like we had more than we did. She had come from a fairly wealthy family and she just didn't know how to economize very well, especially if it was something my brother or I wanted or needed. Now what we wanted we didn't always need, but she would buy it for us anyway.

Her worst transgression was the purchase of a tape recorder. Now, I don't mean a handheld recorder like you can have today; this was a recorder that sat in a box on a table and weighed a ton. For some reason my brother had seen it and wanted it, and she bought it. Now what would a ten-year-old boy need with a sixty-dollar tape recorder? I still don't know the answer to that one.

My Daddy was a mild-mannered man but he lost it when he saw the tape recorder. He blew up. It had to go back. My mother just let him have his say. Then she began to explain what an educational enhancer it was. It would help both of us boys be better students, etc, etc, etc. He didn't buy her argument, but he did end up buying the tape recorder. When the bill came he paid it, and to be truthful my brother did use that thing for his studies.

I never used it. I thought it was stupid to talk into a machine, or to record something you had already heard. Plus, it had caused an argument and I didn't like arguments. I liked my life to be simple and uncomplicated. That is why I liked Holland Street and Clinton so much. If any place was simple and uncomplicated it was Clinton.

It truly did seem like I lived in a bubble and the outside world never intruded. I never saw a race riot, a bank robbery, or a theft of any kind. We did have one murder in town but it was quickly hushed up and life got back to normal. The preacher I had at the First Baptist Church was there for twenty-something years and the mayor of our town was elected to four consecutive terms. It was a stable and consistent place to live.

Many people would have been bored out of their minds to live in such a quiet town, but not me. When my friends talked about wanting to get out and get away, I thought they were crazy. I liked living in a small town. I liked knowing most of the people who lived there. It was my town and I was proud of it.

I don't go back to Clinton very often these days. It is still pretty much the same as far as layout, but the faces and families have changed. I prefer to remember it as it was. It was a town that time forgot, but it lives forever in my memory.

The Gift of Laughter

It is not easy to make me laugh. I like to laugh, but not too many people can make me laugh. One who can is Judge George Nunn. Now George can be deadly serious. He can be, well, sober as a judge, but he can also be hilariously funny. If he weren't content being a judge, he could probably make a good living playing comedy clubs around the country.

Years ago my wife and I were part of a group that played bridge on a regular basis. George and his wife Janet were also part of that group. I loved playing cards, but what I enjoyed most was listening to George. He could have me crying because I laughed so much.

The other day at church George told me a story that was pure George. By the time he finished I was laughing so hard I could hardly stand it.

George said he was at a Rotary meeting a few months ago. There was a pretty big crowd there and everyone was sitting around talking before the meeting started. When it did start, the person presiding noticed there was a piano in the room with them. She stated that they ought to sing some songs if anyone could play the piano, and then asked for a volunteer. George raised his hand.

As soon as he raised his hand he heard the mumbling begin. "Can he play?" someone asked. "No, he can't play," said another. And on the mumbling went even as George stood and started for the piano.

George said he walked slowly and listened as the conversation turned to "Well you know his daughter plays." And then it was added, "And you know he comes from a musical family. So maybe..." George said by the time he sat down at the piano all doubt had been erased and now everyone was beginning to think he could play the piano.

He then asked if anyone had a request. "Play 'God Bless America,'" someone shouted. Another asked for "America, the Beautiful." George settled on "God Bless America." He raised his arms, flexed his fingers, and let them come down soundly on the piano keys. It was horrible.

"I can't play on this piano," George said. "It is definitely out of tune." And with that he rose and went back to his seat.

I love this story. First, it shows George's good sense of humor, and second, it shows he can poke fun at himself. Third, it is a testament to his wicked wit.

If you ever get the chance, and George is in the mood, get him to tell you some of his stories. I guarantee they will leave you laughing. They always have with me.

A Literary Festival

The first annual Heart of Georgia Literary Festival will be held this month in Macon, Georgia. This event is being organized to showcase writers of Middle Georgia. It also offers an opportunity for aspiring writers to come and "pick the minds" of those who have already had some success in their field.

Writers come in all colors, ages, shapes and sizes. They are lawyers, doctors, housewives, civil servants, and any other type of person you can imagine. They all have stories inside their souls that are just waiting to burst on to the printed page. And when they are released, well that is a beautiful sight to see.

I have always loved to read. I don't know why I had that gift, or where it came from. My parents were not readers, but my brother and I were. When I read books as a child I read for the content only. I didn't have any idea of what went into the writing process, or that there were people around me who could write. That all came later.

One of the first authors I ever met was William Diehl. I did a story on him for *Georgia Journal* magazine and had to go to St. Simons Island to interview him. Diehl is the author of *Sharkey's Machine*, *Primal Fear*, and *Eureka* among others. He is a gifted speaker (which all authors are not) and a gifted storyteller. I was impressed by him to no end and have read every book he has ever written. It also amazes me that at age seventy-eight he is still talking about his next novel.

Another author I admire is Jaclyn Weldon White. She is the author of *Whisper to the Black Candle* and *The Empty Nursery*. These are both true crime stories about events that happened in

Georgia. Jackie White now lives in Macon, Georgia, and is one of the brightest and most personable authors I have ever met.

When you read her two books you are stuck with the ugliness of the crimes committed, but somehow Jackie White manages to ensure that heart and the promise of happiness are also present. The world is a place of sin and crime but in Jackie's books there is always that ray of hope and faith.

My very favorite author is Pat Conroy. He is to me the true epitome of what a Southern writer (or any writer) should be. His stories are huge and sprawling with a lush description of some Southern locale always anchoring them. After I read *The Lords of Discipline*, I was hooked for life. If you have never read the book, you can't know what a magnificent saga it is.

I have started a radio show each Saturday morning from eleven till noon. On this show I talk about movies and videos, but I also talk about books. I have been lucky enough to get some authors to talk with me on air. I have had William Diehl, Eileen Goudge, and Sandra Chastain on my show so far. This week I hope to talk with Michael Connelly who wrote *Blood Work* and has a new book out called *Chasing the Dime*.

Since I talk with these people by phone they usually agree to take a few minutes to discuss their books. Coming up are William Harris, Evan Hunter, Jeffrey Deaver, and Frances Mayes. And I'm pursuing Pat Conroy. I haven't gotten a "yes" out of him yet, but I am on his trail. Wish me luck!

A College Homecoming

Last week I went back to visit Erskine College, the college I attended in South Carolina. It was the first time I had been back in over twenty years. I always intended to visit, but somehow the time slipped away and the days and years passed by. But for this homecoming weekend I had been invited to come back to Erskine and be part of a group of authors being recognized.

I had been back one other time since I graduated and that was for a class reunion. It was right after Terry and I had gotten married. The class reporter wrote in the *Erskine Alumni Magazine* that I must have married a good cook as I looked so "healthy." This time when I went back no one mentioned my "health."

Terry and I went to Greenwood, South Carolina, and spent the night. The next morning, we drove over to Due West, South Carolina, where Erskine is located. As we got close to Erskine, the morning mists were just coming off the fields. As the world unfolded, it reminded me of "Brigadoon." Just like that town rose magically out of the mists, so on this morning did Erskine.

A lot of things had changed at Erskine, but most things had stayed the same. There are some new buildings, such as the Bowie Arts Center where the book signings were held. But the men's campus and the women's campus are still on opposite sides of the town. No coed dorms here! And the students still have a squeaky-clean look to them for the most part.

As I met people who had come to Erskine for homecoming, I was asked over and over where I was born. When I answered that I was born in Clinton, this started off a whole conversation of "Do you know so and so?" It seems I was definitely related to at least half the people there.

For the few hours I was there, I felt I was in the land that time forgot. It all had a sixties feel to it, and even my wife said it was like time had stood still in so many ways. As I talked with the people who lived there and worked there I felt myself slipping back to the attitudes we had all held when we attended the school. It was an easier pace and a more considerate time.

I am sure there are some modern elements alive and well at Erskine today, but the view I had of the school and town was still that of a place dedicated to certain religious beliefs and standards. It is a place you want to believe exists even if your mind doubts that it can.

As we were driving back to Georgia from Due West, I imagined the mists coming up once again and taking the town away for another twenty-year sleep. Then it will awaken once more and still be the place it was and always will be.

The Conroy Connection

When I was growing up in Clinton, South Carolina, my best friend was Tommy Sublett. I first met him when he would come to visit his grandparents who lived in Clinton. Tommy and I were something like fourth cousins and that is how we got to know each other. His mother was a Hollis and my Daddy knew all his Hollis relatives.

Tommy was from Kentucky but moved to Clinton when we were in the seventh grade. I remember him coming to my school, but I don't remember when we became good friends. It was something that just happened. In high school Tommy lived to play basketball. It was the end all, be all to him. He not only loved to play the game, he loved to listen to the game, especially those games involving the University of Kentucky team. He would tune in on his radio to the Louisville station and listen in rapt adoration as Coach Adolph Rupp steered his team to glory.

I, who couldn't care less about basketball, learned the name of Adolph Rupp and back then even knew some of the members of the Kentucky team. They were the idols of Tommy's world and occasionally I would join him in tuning in and entering the shrine.

In the tenth grade, Tommy played on the varsity basketball team when underclassmen were not supposed to. He was not a tall person in those days, but he played with more heart and spirit than anyone else in the school. In our junior year he played on a team made up of mostly seniors and he lived for each and every game. When they won, his spirits soared and when they lost it crumbled.

As for me, I could have cared less about the game. I went to watch him play just because he was my friend. It was only years later when I talked to some of my old classmates that I truly realized how good he was at the game.

What Tommy did convey to me was how much he loved it all. He was never happier than when he was on the court with the four other guys playing as a team. He would try to explain to me how much it meant to him to be good at the game, and how good it felt when his team connected and they all played as one unit.

I wanted to enter into this world, just because Tommy said how wonderful it was. This led me to practice the entire summer before my senior year and then go out for the team as a senior. Now, if life were a movie, I would have made the team and been a fairly successful player. But life isn't a movie, and I didn't make the team. I just got to suffer the humiliation of not being selected. I cringe even now as I write about it, even after all these years.

Recently, I read Pat Conroy's new book *My Losing Season*. It's all about his senior year and his life as a basketball player for the Citadel. With the mastery of his words, he finally revealed to me what Tommy Sublett loved about the game and about being part of a team. This book lifted the veil and after half a lifetime the mystery was solved.

I'm still not an avid sports fan, but finally I do see why people are. I am going to give Tommy Sublett a copy of *My Losing Season*. He and Conroy are brothers at heart through their love of the game. My best friend and my favorite writer should get to know each other.

The Blessing of George

When I was assigned to the Staff Judge Advocate's Office at Robins Air Force Base many years ago, one of the first people I met was Leonard Grace. The JAG Office gave advice on personnel matters and Leonard worked in the Civilian Personnel Office. And when you met Leonard you immediately learned about his wife Ann and their son George.

Leonard and Ann had only been blessed with one child, but when that child fulfilled all their dreams as George did, well, they truly were blessed. They adored him; he adored them. It was a mutual admiration society of the best kind.

As George grew he remained everything Leonard and Ann could want in a son. He was personable and he was talented. Eventually after graduating from college, George got a job at Robins Air Force Base, but he also participated in musical functions on the side. He was a member of the Minstrel Singers; he played in various orchestras, and he served as a choir director for different churches.

I had kept up with George through Leonard, but when he became choir director at Christ Methodist Church I got to know him more personally than ever before. My wife is director of the school at Christ Methodist Church so she and George attended staff meetings and other church activities together.

Two Christmases ago, my wife Terry and I attended the staff Christmas party, which was held at the home of George and his wife Gwen. George was his usual cheerful self and I felt pleased to get to know Gwen and their son Wesley. After we left I thought how strange it was that I had gotten to be friends with both generations of the Grace family. When I first met Leonard Grace, I was bowled over by his enthusiasm for life. He was one of the most outgoing and gregarious human beings I ever met. George had the same enthusiasm for life but in a more subdued way. His passion was music and he created it beautifully through his choir.

There was also a sensitivity to George and this came from his mother Ann. He was a good soul, you could feel it when you met him. His warmth and his total humanity were out there for anyone to see.

Last Christmas, I attended one of the Christmas concerts which George's choir gave. It was a wonderful night, full of great music and true Christmas cheer. George directed the choir with enthusiasm, and his love for what he did was evident in every movement of his hands and every beat of his foot.

It was only a few months later that I learned that George was suffering from cancer. He started treatments, but the prognosis was not good. Shortly thereafter, I began to receive e-mails from Leonard that gave updates on George's progress. There was a large address list for these e-mails and I know all the others appreciated them as much as I did.

All through the summer Leonard kept me informed as to how George was doing and how he and Ann were holding up. They had their moments of hope and they had their moments of depression, but through it all their faith in God never wavered. Each message contained an affirmation of their beliefs.

As I read these messages, I marveled at how Leonard maintained his own composure. I thought that had I been in his shoes I surely would have just lost my mind. But with each message he remained hopeful, faithful, and loving of his son. He was a father being torn apart but holding it all together for George, other members of his family, and his friends.

On Sunday, October 27, I got an e-mail from Leonard titled "George Promoted to Eternal Life." I grieve for George's family and especially his father and mother, but I know he is in a better place. He lived his life like the name he bore. For all his too short time on this earth, he was a person full of grace.

The Political Scene

I know that in a few weeks the elections will be over. And none too soon for me. I am tired of the phone calls, tired of the ads, tired of the commercials. I am "politicked off."

When I was growing up in Clinton, South Carolina, the first politician I remember being aware of was the mayor of our town. His name was Peck Cornwall and his daughter, Lou Jones, was my age. Peck was mayor forever and never had any opposition when he ran. He was a Clinton institution until the day he died.

The other politician I knew growing up was Strom Thurmond. Somehow he and my Uncle Russell were friends. Whenever my family needed something done, my father would always say he could talk to Russell who could talk to Strom.

To my knowledge the only time we actually used this connection was when I was in law school and the draft was breathing down my neck. Daddy talked to Russell who talked to Strom Thurmond and the draft board got off my back. (At least until after I got out of school and passed the Bar. I joined the Air Force the next day.)

Strom Thurmond is still a part of the South Carolina political scene. He isn't running this year, but in all the other years he rarely had any strong opposition. Nobody wanted to mess with Strom.

I tell you all this to show that I didn't grow up being a political person. I still am not. And when I am, it is about the person and not the party. But lately I have begun to have friends who are running for elected office so I am more drawn into the murky waters of the campaigns. I don't like how this makes me feel.

The ads for the political races have been the worst ever this year. I cringe when I see rats crawling over the capitol, and I flinch when I hear some other candidate called a liar. I want to hear about the good ideas and the progressive values. I don't want to hear "Vote for me because I am better than that snake in the grass."

When the election is over I hope we can get back to making this a better, safer, more tolerant country. The country we all still dream about and hope we can be. I want to feel safe from terrorists. I want to feel the economy is going to get better. I want to think that honest, moral people are in the Senate and the House.

The election will soon be over but in two years it will be back again. When it returns I hope it is with candidates who have a more positive attitude and who place the emphasis on what good things can be done by them, and not by what wrong things have been done by their opposition.

God bless the politicians. I wouldn't have their jobs. I wouldn't subject myself and my family to the rigors and horrors of a campaign. But luckily some people are willing to meet the challenge. And in some instances they even have the right motives.

She Lights up My Life

Whenever she arrives the world brightens up! It is amazing how much love one little two-year-old child can inspire. Just let her come to visit and all my troubles fly away as I focus on my granddaughter Genna and her world.

This past week she came to visit for a few days and she had just gotten her hair cut. She patted the sides of her head and declared it was "just beautiful." And it is. It is red and special and just as beautiful as can be. I didn't realize there aren't that many redheaded people in the world. They are the exception rather than the rule and I now notice the ones who are.

We have gotten Genna a dollhouse and she loves it. As soon as she comes into our house she heads upstairs where her "doll family" lives. We sit there for the longest times moving the dolls around the rooms and having conversations. They seem so real to her, and through her eyes, they become real to me.

My wife Terry and I were sitting there with Genna the other morning. She was having a wonderful time, and my wife was enhancing it all with her ability to make the dolls speak. I go along with it all, but I am not as good at this as is my wife Terry. She is amazing in helping Genna create a world for the dolls and toys.

As we played, I said, "You are Nana's girl, aren't you?" because she so obviously is. But Genna shook her head and said, "No. I'm not."

Terry looked at her and said, "You aren't Nana's girl?" Genna shook her head again and turned to me and said, "I am his girl." That's it hook, line, and sinker. Reel me in. She lit up my world. She is my girl and always will be.

But as I thought those thoughts, I also thought of little Terrence Smith. He is the baby boy of some friends of ours, and is just about the same exact age as my grandson Walker. Terrence has some serious medical problems and his life has become quite a struggle.

In the same way that Genna is my girl, Terrence is my boy. He belongs to all of us. I think God entrusts children to us all. They may not be born to us, but they are a part of us. And Terrence needs my help. He needs my prayers and he needs my support in other ways. He is just a baby and babies shouldn't have to worry about liver transplants and so on—and neither should their parents.

We all have a child in our lives who has captured our heart. For the love we have for them, let's all say a prayer for those who may not be as healthy as our own are. Genna and Walker own my heart, but there is room there for concern for all the sick children like Terrence. They light up someone's life, too.

A Foundation in Church

Whenever I think back on my childhood, one of the most constant images is being in church with my mother and father. Strangely, though, I never see my brother in the picture. I know he was there. He was always there. Half the town thought Tommy Cooper was going to grow up to be a minister. Little did they know that Jackie Cooper's second-born son would be the minister in the family.

The First Baptist Church of Clinton was a huge church. The sanctuary was round and there was a sliding wall that could be removed, revealing additional pews. When the crowds grew large, and they often did, the ushers would raise the sliding wall to seat the people in those pews.

During my teenage years, my crowd and I always sat in the "added" section. When I sat with my parents, we sat in the tenth row of the center section. That was the Cooper pew and had been for years. It was right under one of the overhead fans and some of the best sleep I ever had was on that hard pew.

On summer mornings, the sun came in through the stained glass window depicting Jesus praying in Gethsemane. Where we sat, the scarlet of his robe would play across my mother's face. She never squinted her eyes at the effect but sat there shining as brightly as could be with the scarlet blending with the red highlights of her hair.

Church on Sunday morning was the perfect way to start the week. It gave a completeness to all that had happened the days before, and it gave an anticipation to whatever was to come.

Sunday was the only day my father didn't work. Just like God, he rested on the Sabbath.

Whenever I need peace in my soul and my life, I think back to my days at the First Baptist Church in Clinton. Brother Joseph Darr was the preacher there and it was he who baptized me. Annette Henderson directed the choir and her soft ways and gentle spirit infused the hymns with a soothing effect.

The church was my strength and my refuge. I always felt secure within its walls, and I always sensed that there was a power centered there that could solve my problems and lift my burdens. It was there I went after my mother died. I sat alone in the sanctuary and put all my grief and guilt on someone else.

Through the years, I have belonged to other churches and now I even belong to a new denomination. My Baptist days have ended. I am a true blue Methodist. But in a corner of my heart I still hold on to the warmth and peace of First Baptist Church. It was where I learned about God and where I accepted my faith.

As an adult I accept the fact that churches are not perfect. I have seen them torn apart by arguments and differences; I have seen them lifted by renewals and redemption. The only church that is perfect is the one in my memory. It is one I see through a child's eyes. It is the one that will be waiting for me when I get to Heaven.

Death of a Friend

It is hard to write the words "last week a friend of mine died," but it's true. I lost my friend Ann Conner Storey and her death came much too early to one much too young to die. But death comes unannounced to us and it matters not what your age or your status is.

I have been friends with Ann just about the entire twenty-five years I have lived in Perry. Her sister, Abbie Sue Ginn, lived next to my wife and me when we lived on Forest Avenue in our first house. It was a place where life was simple and enjoyable. I spent many hours sitting in a lawn chair talking with Abbie Sue. We didn't discuss anything in particular, but just let the day wind down.

When Abbie Sue and her husband John decided to move up near Atlanta, we went over to their house to say goodbye. That is when I first met Ann. She was there to help pack things up. My main recollection of her at that time was that she had this Audrey Hepburn thing going in that she seemed so vulnerable. She also brought out the protective older brother feelings in me.

Through the years, I would see Ann from time to time. She always made me feel good as she appreciated my sense of humor. We always laughed when we talked, and that is a good test of friendship in any situation.

Last week, Terry and I spent a few days in Lake Junaluska, North Carolina, with my former pastor Larry Roberts and his wife Myrna. I had been invited to speak to the Junaluskans, a group to which Larry and Myrna belong. After I gave my talk that

Tuesday night, Terry and I went back to the Roberts home and sat in their living room talking about Perry.

I told Larry that one of my best memories of his ministry was a Bible Study he held in the parsonage. A small group of us attended it and those who were involved became very close. I mentioned that I became better friends with Ann Conner because of that Bible study. She had been a part of the group and seemed to enjoy it immensely.

Myrna and Ann had worked together at the Chamber of Commerce. She asked how Ann was doing now and I responded that I really didn't know. I hadn't seen her in some time and I needed to check on her and see how she was doing. Little did I know that as we sat there talking it was already too late to check on Ann.

Terry and I came back home in the middle of the week and I learned that Ann had died over the weekend. I can't say that I was totally surprised. Her vulnerability had finally caught up with her.

Some people sail through life with only an occasional trouble here or there. Not so with Ann. For her, life was difficult. God didn't assign her a free ride in any way. Instead of seeing blue skies, she had to contend with storms. Still, she waged a good fight. During the years of our friendship, I would see her at times when I knew she was at her most depressed. The aura around her would be one of hopelessness. Still, when we would speak you could see her summoning up her courage to overcome whatever had caused her heartache. She was a slight little thing, but she was also one of the strongest people I ever met.

I will miss my friend Ann. I will miss her personality and her intensity. I will miss that protective spirit she inspired in me. For all the time I knew her she remained a unique individual.

Rest in peace now, Ann, rest in peace.

Here Come the Holidays

Well, Thanksgiving is over and here comes Christmas. It is hard for me to believe that it is that time of the year again. If having time go faster is a sign of getting older, then Methuselah and I have a lot in common. It honestly seems like it was summer last week.

This was a good Thanksgiving for me and my family. Both of my boys were home as well as my daughter-in-law and grandchildren. We ate ourselves silly on Thanksgiving, and then celebrated further by playing Trivial Pursuit. This is one of my favorite games to play because if anyone knows "trivia" it is I. I was pumped up and ready to go.

My wife watched the grandkids so Paula, Sean, JJ, and I could play in teams: Paula and JJ against Sean and me. Sean and I took a roaring lead at the start. We were answering questions right and left. JJ and Paula just couldn't get it together. I smugly knew the game was in the bag.

But then things changed. Sean and I hit a dry spell. We couldn't answer a one, but suddenly JJ and Paula were getting everything right. I was positive they were just guessing, pure and simple. But they were the right guesses. It was a disaster in the making, and sure enough, we lost.

Immediately, we demanded a rematch. We fortified ourselves with brain food: soft drinks and chips. We were seriously into it this time. The game started and almost immediately it ended, or so it seemed. They flew around that board getting pieces of pie right and left. They won again.

It was humiliating. Still, the torch has obviously passed. My reign as trivia king is over. JJ, Sean, and Paula knew many more of the answers to the questions concerning musical groups, current history, and above all else sports, than I did. I felt like a failure.

Still, my kids loved me because the next morning they got up at 5:00 A.M. and went to Wal-Mart for the big computer sale. I had agreed to be on the radio from seven till nine so I had to leave for Macon while they were still at the store. When I got back home, I had a new computer system all set up. Now, I am a man of simple pleasures and having a new computer (which is my Christmas present) was a real thrill.

As the holiday gathering progressed, my house began to shrink. We have a two-story, four-bedroom home and that has always seemed like plenty of space, but not anymore. We took one bedroom, JJ took another, Genna was in hers, and Walker has his own room, too. That left the downstairs sofas for Sean and Paula. JJ offered to let them have his room but they insisted they would be fine downstairs.

At Christmastime, they will all be back plus my stepmother. I guess I had better get busy adding some more rooms, or at least seeing about some sleeping bags. But whatever it takes for us all to be together will be worth it. I truly believe that holidays are all about family. It isn't a trip to a resort or a condo on the beach; it's just having your kids and their kids home with you.

I used to sort through things to make my list of what I am thankful for on this holiday. Now it's simple. I always just think of family. That one word says it all.

My Gal Bobbie Is Back

Bobbie is back! Bobbie Eakes that is. Several years ago, she signed up to play Macy Alexander on the popular TV soap *The Bold and the Beautiful*. She was on the show for several years but suddenly, about two and a half years ago, she was killed off. Well, her character supposedly died in a car wreck, *but* the body was never found.

Last week they announced on the show that Macy was back. They haven't explained it all yet, but it seems as if she has had amnesia or something and has been living in Portofino, Italy. She now goes by the name of Lena, and as Bobbie told me, sings a lot of songs in Italian. Now Bobbie doesn't speak Italian but she does have a good ear, so it all sounds authentic.

For those of you who are reading this and don't know who Bobbie Eakes is (and what rock have you been living under?), she is the daughter of Mr. and Mrs. Robert Eakes of Warner Robins and is one of their five daughters. Bobbie first gained fame through the Warner Robins High School Follies and then went on to become Miss Georgia.

She moved to Hollywood to pursue a singing and acting career and the rest is history. In addition to coming back to *The Bold and Beautiful*, she also just completed a movie titled *Charlie's War*, co-starring Olympia Dukakis, Lynn Redgrave, and Diane Ladd. Now, that is some cast.

A few years ago Bobbie married writer David Steen. They were wed at the Robins Air Force Base chapel and my wife and I went to the wedding. Several of Bobbie's castmates from *The Bold and the Beautiful* flew in for the occasion and that was a real compliment to her. I mean Warner Robins is far from Hollywood even in this day of easy air travel.

Last year Bobbie recorded a fantastic duet with Colin Raye. The title of the song was "I'm Tired of Loving This Way." Her voice had never sounded better and in the video of the song she looked gorgeous. It was pretty popular, but it should have reached number one on the charts!

The amazing thing about Bobbie is that each time I talk with her she is still the nice sweet person she was when I first met her. She has never "gone Hollywood" and luckily enough the guy she married is just as nice as she is. Plus his parents are extra special people. I met them at the wedding and they fit in just as easy as could be with us Georgia folks.

I love it when people from our area make it big in Hollywood. Blake Clarke from Macon was on the *Home Improvement* show with Tim Allen and can be seen in just about every movie Adam Sandler makes. Victor Brown from Warner Robins is a successful actor who has a new show coming on the Sci-Fi Channel. It is called "Tremors" and it is based on the movie of the same name. Victor has the Kevin Bacon role.

But the brightest star of them all is Bobbie Eakes. We can all tune in and see her every day on ""B&B." She will be acting and singing and letting that grand personality shine through. She is one of us who made it big. Now we can vicariously have Hollywood success through her.

Welcome back, Bobbie. "The Bold and the Beautiful" has missed you and so have we!

The Best Christmas Ever

Can you believe Christmas is here again? It was just a few months ago that we were celebrating it, or so it seems. This year I just wasn't ready for it to get here. There were supposed to be lots of shopping days between Thanksgiving and now. Where did they go?

This is going to be one of the best Christmases ever. The reason is that my granddaughter Genna is almost three and I will get to see Christmas through her eyes. She is already talking about what Santa is going to bring her and her brother Walker. Being able to see her face when she actually gets her presents, well, that will be worth everything.

I also think that seeing Christmas through her eyes reminds me that the holiday isn't just about presents. It is about the wonder and the awe of the day. A spirit of love and fellowship comes into our lives during this special time of the year that should be there year round but isn't.

Christmas is a time for miracles. Even if you don't believe in them 364 other days, you must believe in them on Christmas Day. And boy do we need them now. With the world on the brink of war and enmities accelerating, can't we use a miracle to calm things down? Wouldn't it be nice to get just a small measure of security in our lives? I think at this time of the year it can happen. So I pray for miracles.

I also want miracles for all the people who are suffering from horrendous illnesses. I want them to be cured, and if not cured then at least given peace of mind and soul. It seems this year I have heard about more of my friends having terrible sicknesses than at any other time in my life. Maybe it is my age and the fact my friends are getting older, but some of the bad things are happening to really young friends of mine. So I pray for miracles.

Some of my friends are facing career challenges. It might be that they want to change careers, or maybe their careers have left them. Jobs have been lost and money depleted. I always think it can't happen to me or mine, but it can. It has happened to those who are close to me. The security of a job and a paycheck are there one day and gone the next. So I pray for miracles.

My church is my refuge, the place where I restore my faith and renew my commitment. It is God's place and is there to serve him. But ordinary people worship there, and try to run it for him. Sometimes they make mistakes and sometimes they forget why they are there. I don't like harsh words in my church. I don't like threats and bitterness. I think people should always remember they are there for God and to serve his will. But human beings lead imperfect lives and words can be said that hurt. It happens. It shouldn't, but it does. So I pray for miracles.

Christmas is when people should be at their best. They should be at their most loving and caring. They should be full of good cheer and good will. They should put aside their pettiness and their meanness and do good things.

So if you are entering the Christmas season with hard feelings or ill will towards someone, shouldn't you remember what time of year it is and change? That makes sense to me. I hope it does to you. After all it is the season of miracles. And if we can become better so can the world.

A Christmas Surprise

From the very first Christmas that I can remember, when I was asked what I wanted Santa Claus to bring me, I answered, "A surprise!" Now you can imagine what that did to my family. They reminded me that Santa needed a clue. But I wouldn't budge. I wanted a surprise and that was it.

Then on Christmas morning I would wake up, go into the living room, and announce I didn't get my surprise. Then I turned on my heels and went back to bed. Talk about a rotten kid; I was the poster child back then.

When I was fourteen years old my mother died never having had the pleasure of giving me "my surprise." Lord knows she had tried. She had asked me constantly what my surprise would be, and I had stuck with the fact that although I didn't know what it was, I would know it when I got it.

At least as I got older, I quit talking about the surprise. I *did* have that much sense. But inside I still had that hunger for the unknown present that would make me feel satisfied. Christmases came and went and I still felt I was missing out on something undefined.

When I went off to college I selected Erskine College in Due West, South Carolina. It was an Associate Reformed Presbyterian school, but a lot of my high school classmates chose to go there and I did, too. My Baptist father wondered why I hadn't chosen Furman.

Anyway, one of the highlights of the Christmas season was buying a gift for a child from a nearby orphanage. My best friend at the school was all involved in it and he convinced me to join in too.

A month or so before Christmas a group of children, mainly the new kids to the orphanage, were brought over and introduced to us "sponsors." We got to choose the child we wanted. I chose a little girl named Virginia, because that is my mother's name. The lady from the orphanage who came with them told me Virginia was not a child who talked much or demonstrated affection; she was an abused child.

While I was in college, my father sent me five dollars a week. That was the money I used to date, buy cokes, etc. Now, five dollars went further back then, but it still wasn't a lot of money. It seemed even less when I saw a doll that I thought Virginia would like—and it cost eleven dollars. Still, I managed to scrimp and save and get the money, and get the doll.

When the day arrived to give the presents, I didn't know what to expect. I didn't know if Virginia would like the doll, especially since I had no sisters and was clueless as to what was "in" for little girls that year. So I was apprehensive as she unwrapped the box.

When she saw what it was her face lit up. She clutched it to her, and then put it aside as she came over and reached up and hugged my neck. I heard the woman who was with them saying to someone, "Well, now that's a surprise!"

Then and there I had my epiphany. It was the surprise I had been waiting for all my life. And all it took was giving instead of getting.

I hope you got your "surprise" this Christmas, and I hope it came because you gave as well as received.

Reflections from Route 2003

My Buddy Brandon

A few days before Christmas, I was contacted by my friend Gayle Borah and asked if I would speak to her son Brandon's sixth-grade class at Westfield. She just wanted me to tell them a couple of Christmas stories and I quickly agreed to do it. I like kids and I am always ready to talk.

So the Friday before Christmas, I spoke to her class. The three teachers, Ms. Harrell, Ms. Huckabee, and Ms. Lee, met me when I entered the facility. As I already knew all of these teachers, I was perfectly comfortable; then the kids started coming in.

Julie Harrell had asked her student Brandon to introduce me, so Julie, Brandon, and I stood before the group and Brandon started telling his class about me. "He writes a column for the paper," he said. "And he is in my mom and dad's Sunday School class."

At this point he hesitated, so I leaned over and prompted him. "He's very nice," I whispered.

"He's very nice," said Brandon.

"He's very handsome," I whispered.

"He's very handsome," said Brandon.

"He has a lot of hair," I whispered.

"He has—." Brandon choked on that one. He just couldn't get that one said without cracking up.

Anyway, I told two stories to a group of kids who were courteous and responsive to the stories. Afterwards, they gathered around and asked questions. The girls were impressed when I said I had met Brittney Spears and Ben Affleck. The boys didn't act impressed with anything.

As I got ready to leave they presented me with a huge caramel cake. I love caramel cake! And this one was all for me. I couldn't have asked for a better gift.

That afternoon I was signing copies of my book at the Olive Branch in Warner Robins. A young boy, about twelve years old, came up to me and told me he had been in the group I talked to that morning. He told me he had liked my stories.

As he walked away, I thanked him for coming up to speak to me. He turned around, grinned, and thanked me for coming out to talk to his class. I was impressed by his poise and his friendliness. When I was twelve, it would have been a big thing for me to walk up to a relative stranger and make conversation. But he did it easily. This new generation is okay.

The holidays have passed. The caramel cake is gone. But the memories of that morning linger on.

Ah, She's Adorable

She's three years old! It's amazing, that's what it is. At this rate, my granddaughter Genna will be grown before I know it. It is like watching a movie on fast forward.

I had worried that she would miss out on a real birthday feeling since her birthday comes so close to Christmas, but I will worry no more. She had a birthday spend the night with her best friend Hannah on the actual birthday of January 7. Then on Friday my wife took her to the school where she is the director, and Genna had a birthday party there.

On Saturday, we traveled to Moultrie along with Genna's other grandparents and three sets of aunts and uncles and had another birthday party. The next day, she had seven friends in for another party. Plus, she had yet another one on Tuesday at her school in Moultrie where she goes twice a week. I don't think any little girl has ever been as celebrated.

But she didn't get the holiday/birthday gene from Sean and me. He and I have that awful "we don't like things out of the ordinary" gene that kicks into overdrive when there is a holiday, birthday, or some other unusual event. Our girl Genna loved every minute of celebrating, and she oohed and aahed over each and every gift just as we wanted her to do.

Watching her at three is like watching a mystery unfold. You never know what her mood will be—she doesn't have red hair for nothing. Her mood can shift in a flash and she can go from adoring you to shunning you in an instant. Still, when you're the center of attention with her, it is heaven on earth.

On Thursday night when she came up to stay with us so she could go to her party at Terry's school on Friday, I was the man of the moment. She wanted me beside her as she watched *Scooby-Doo* and *Cinderella*. And nothing could have been sweeter than having her curl up beside me on the sofa and drift off to sleep.

The next morning, Terry brought her into our room so she could have some snuggling time before she went off to school. Once again she just wanted to be close to me, and kiss me, and hug me.

But at other times, she can be fiercely independent and want to be alone, or with only Terry. During those times she is Nana's girl and Pooh can just get away. You just have to accept that she is the "princess" and you only get to have her favor when she wants to bestow it.

At Christmas, my stepmother Florence came to stay with us for a few days. She hadn't seen Genna in a year and I was nervous that Genna might not want to have anything to do with this great-grandmother she didn't really know. I still get nervous about Florence's feelings and try to do everything to keep her in a good mood.

When Genna came in the back door in Sean's arms, I went up to her and she immediately said "No, Pooh. Get away!" Sean explained that she wasn't in the best mood. I could see tragedy looming in my future as Florence came into the room. But the mood changed in a split second. Sean let her down and she went up to Florence and cooed, "Hello, grandmother, how are you? My name is Genna and this is my doll Shoo Shoo." She did everything but curtsey, and of course Florence declared she was the most wonderful little girl in the world.

She is wonderful and she is my Genna. Because of her, I love her parents even more because they gave her to us. And I love Terry more because she shares my love for her. And I love

Genna's little brother Walker more because he is just as wonderful in his way as she is in hers. And I love her Uncle J.J. more because he lights up every time he sees her or even just talks about her.

She has her own mind and she has all our hearts. She is our own special princess who is three going on thirty, and she has claimed us all as her royal and loyal subjects.

Six Degrees of Celebrity Separation

It still amazes me that I get to meet celebrities. Although I have been reviewing movies and meeting various stars of one kind or another for over twenty years, I am still in awe of any form of famous personage. Last week I had another first. I interviewed a Pulitzer Prize winner.

Author Michael Cunningham was in Atlanta to help publicize the film *The Hours*, starring Meryl Streep, Nicole Kidman, and Julianne Moore. That's not a bad cast for any movie, but a very good one for a film that boasts three strong female roles. The film is based on Cunningham's 1998 Pulitzer Prize-winning novel.

Cunningham is fifty years old but looks younger. He is friendly and not at all aloof. He seemed to be having a good time talking about his book. For the thirty minutes or more that we talked, we spent most of the time laughing.

It started when I asked him how it felt to win the Pulitzer. He said it was a wonderful and unexpected honor. But then he added, "You know it isn't that great looking. It is more of a knick-knack than a trophy. I expected something like the Heismann. The Pulitzer is more of a door stop."

Shocked at that description, I had to ask him about the monetary prize. Greedy me wanted to know if it was a lot of money. "Not really," he said. "Not a lot. But it is a big honor and it is nice to have that identification after your name."

So there you have it folks, the Pulitzer is a knick-knack of an award that doesn't bring the winner a lot of cash. I had thought it was like the Nobel Peace Prize where we're talking big bucks. At least, Jimmy Carter got a cool million when he won the Nobel.

As my conversation with Cunningham continued, he mentioned that his next book was going to be an interweaving of three novellas. One would be a science fiction story, one would be a Gothic romance, and one would be a thriller, and they would all interrelate to each other.

Since *The Hours* is a story about three different women in three different decades, I stated that he seemed to be hung up on "threes." "Yes," he answered, "I was talking with Meryl Streep about that last week."

I hooted when he said that, and he got a little flustered. "I guess that did seem a little pretentious," he admitted. "Me dropping Meryl Streep's name like that."

I answered with, "Well now I am going to tell people I was talking with Michael Cunningham last week who was talking with Meryl Streep. And then I can make it a game like that one they play with 'Six Degrees of Kevin Bacon.' To get Jackie Cooper to Kevin Bacon you have Jackie Cooper interviewing Michael Cunningham who wrote *The Hours*, which stars Meryl Streep. And Meryl Streep co-starred in *The River Wild* with Kevin Bacon. Easy as pie!"

On the way back home I listened to a tape of the interview and marveled at how down to earth Cunningham is. I have decided that celebrities are just regular people who have gotten a lucky break and are in the spotlight. They may seem to be a little different than we are because of what they have accomplished but down deep they are just plain old folks like you and me.

Alone but Not Lonely

She is alone now. Alone in the house that she and my father shared for over forty years. She naps during the day and wanders through the rooms at night. It sounds like a bleak existence but in reality it isn't. I think that is because her memories seem more alive at night; and when she is remembering, that is when she is the happiest.

My stepmother, Florence Adair, has always been a part of my life. From my earliest memories she was there. She lived up the street from us and I knew her as a neighbor, a friend of the family, and my best friend Judy's aunt. She was always Florence, not Miss Adair or any nickname, just Florence.

In truth, she and I got along just fine in those early years. Judy and I would go to her house a lot. She lived with her widowed mother for a time; and then after she died, Florence had a series of roommates.

The bad times between us began after my mother died and Florence began dating my father. Then they married and the war began in earnest. I resented her being with my father and being in my house. She resented my very existence, or so it seemed. For years, we didn't speak. We just communicated through my father. I would complain about her to him, and she would complain about me to him.

This battle lasted for almost fifteen years and only ended when I got married and had children. Then the cold war began to thaw. Those times are behind us, but it seems lately that when we talk she wants to go back to them. She wants to explain to me what happened and how things got so out of hand. I would prefer we just let those memories die and concentrate on the good times we shared with my father.

She is really my only link to him. He and my brother Tommy were estranged before his death and didn't really communicate for years before he died. Now when I talk with my brother, he doesn't want to revisit the past. I can't say I blame him but it would be nice to at least talk about the early years before things went sour.

My best conversations with Florence are about my father. We talk for hours about things he said and things he did. He was not a perfect man, but now she has deified him as such. And that is fine. To hear her talk, they were the ideal couple living the ideal life. And maybe they were.

Still, I have to say that she also talks about my mother a lot these days. She talks about their friendship and the fun they shared in the neighborhood. She also tells me stories about my aunts and uncles, all of whom are now gone. Florence is the only living Cooper of that generation of Coopers.

People talk often about how bad it is to get old, and in a lot of ways that is true. But in one way the old have it much better than the young. The old have a wealth of memories; the young do not. And it is those memories that make these so-called "golden years" golden. Florence is alive in the present but her best moments are reliving the past.

In the night, in her home, she talks with my father. She tells me that she does this and that is fine with me. She relives those happiest of times, and what is wrong with that? I worry about her safety, her physical health, and many other things; but I never worry about her happiness. She has enough memories to keep her happy for the rest of her life no matter how long that may be.

Little Things that Drive You Mad

Does this ever happen to you? You go out to get a drink, maybe a diet drink. You go through the drive-through and place your order. Well, you *try* to place your order. The voice from the speaker says, "An eh hop yu?" You hope this is "Can I help you?" and you give your order in return.

"Eh in weow" is the next message and somehow in your brain you translate this jumble to be "second window." So you drive forward, pay your money, and take your drink. You head to the interstate to go to Macon, and as soon as you are cruising that way you pick up your drink. You take a nice long sip and then sputter. Your diet drink is suddenly cherry something and it tastes like cough medicine.

Once again, you are a victim of "let's not get your order right." Are you angry? Oh yeah! Are you enraged? That's right! So what are you going to do about it? Well, if you are like me, you take the first exit and turn around and head back. By the time you get to the fast food place, you are really steamed.

With fire burning in your eyes, you tell the counter person what happened. He/she looks at you with an expression of "so what." Then the words slowly fall out of their mouth. "Sorry," they say and hand you a new drink. Before you can say anything else, they have moved on to another customer, and you are left with the right drink but the wrong attitude.

It seems to me this has happened more and more lately. I place an order and I get my order. If I remember, I look inside the bag and try to ascertain that I got what I ordered. But more times than I like, it turns out the order is wrong. Then I have to stop the car, take the order in, get it changed, and hear a not-too-genuine "sorry!"

Except, a few nights ago my wife got it into her head she wanted some chicken flatbread. I had never heard of that delicacy, but her mind was set. She said it was advertised on TV and it was supposed to be good. Being a good husband, I got in the car and headed to Sam Nunn Boulevard.

I drove through the drive-through, was able to hear "Can I take your order?," and quickly said what I wanted. I moved to the next window and got my order. Everything had been so smooth that I didn't even check it.

When I got home, I rushed into the house and told my wife they actually did have chicken flatbread and handed her the food. She opened the bag, pulled out the contents, and said, "I don't know what this is, but it isn't chicken flatbread." Nope, inside the bag was some kind of barbecue rib looking thing.

My wife, being a trooper, said she would just eat the sandwich. I insisted that I was going to take it back. And I did. I went back to the golden arches and stormed into the main room. I told the pleasant-looking girl at the counter what had happened, and I actually got a genuine sounding apology.

A few seconds later a man I assumed was the manager, brought me my flatbread. As he handed it to me, he said, "I know this doesn't make up for the inconvenience, but I put a couple of apple pies in there too."

Now, I am not a big apple pie eater, but that doesn't matter. He could have put a couple of saltine crackers in there and I would have been impressed. It wasn't that he owed me anything extra; it was the joy of knowing he wanted to make amends for the mistake that had been made.

Those apple pies have made me his friend for life. They have also reinvigorated my faith in my fellow man to do the right thing.

It was just one little sandwich and two apple pies, but it let me know that customer appreciation still exists.

The Storyteller

When I was a child, one of my favorite things was listening to my mother tell stories. Before I went to bed each night, it was story time. Now, some of the ones she would tell would be fun and others would be educational, but most of the ones she told were sad. That was just my mother's nature; she tended to enjoy the sadder stories of life.

What I think this shows that she was a dyed-in-the-wool, true-blue Southerner. Alabama born and raised, she was a Southerner through and through. And Southerners are some of the greatest storytellers around.

Look at the great writers of American literature. Many, many of them are Southern born or adopted the South as their home later in their lives. But from Walker Percy to Eugenia Price, from Flannery O'Connor to William Faulkner, from John Grisham to Anne Rivers Siddons, they dominate the field. And towering above them all is the most Southern of Southern writers, Pat Conroy.

For many, many years I would sit at my mother's feet while she and our neighbors talked. My father would join in the late afternoon sessions, as would other men in the neighborhood. There would always be someone who would say, "Did you hear about.....?" and then the story would be off and running.

Now, some people would call this gossiping, but I prefer to call it storytelling. I do have to admit that some of the stories involved who was running around with whom, but when they started on these, well, that was when I was sent to play with the other kids. I always left reluctantly.

What I did discover in my observations was that most of the more interesting stories involved true occurrences from someone's past. Those were the stories that came most alive in my mind and made me see the narrator from a different perspective from then on. I can still recall those stories and live them over and over in my mind.

I love telling stories. My wife says my life is an open book, and maybe she's right. She always adds that I should keep her book closed, but my kids enjoy me telling stories about them, and my grandchildren haven't voiced any complaints yet.

A few days from now I will be telling my stories at Henderson Village, which is located on the outskirts of Perry and in the village of Henderson. They are presenting A Southern Evening with Jackie K Cooper. It all starts at 6:30 when they will be serving a Southern gourmet meal. I haven't seen the menu, but I know the food will be fantastic!

After the meal, I will start telling some of my stories. They will be some that other people have told me, some that happened to me, and some that happened to my family. I *won't* be telling any stories about my wife: I'll still keep that particular book closed.

Dream It, Believe It, Do It

I am a firm believer in the fact that people can be anything they want to be. This principle was instilled in me by my parents and I tried to instill it in both my boys. I think we are all made as special individuals by God, and if we put our mind to it, we can achieve anything we wish for, no matter how crazy or extreme.

My father was a bread salesman and my mother was a clerk in a store. Neither of them had a college education, but both of them felt strongly about the value of education. My brother and I were never asked if we wanted to attend college. It was a given fact. It was like grades thirteen through sixteen. I would have no more considered not completing those grades than I would have thought of dropping out of high school. It just wasn't an option.

After I had graduated from college and law school and was working for the government at Robins Air Force Base, I was talking with a friend of mine who was a lawyer with one of the biggest firms in Atlanta. He told me if he had it to do all over again he would have been a sports writer. Then he just shrugged it off and said how if he had done that he wouldn't have made the money he was making.

Years later, when he was on his second marriage and rarely saw his children from the first one, he told me he should have changed careers. Being a lawyer is great, he said, but only if you really love it. And he didn't.

For this and other reasons I always told my children that if they decided they were in the wrong professions I would do everything in my power to help them change. Life is much too short to be miserable in any field. I advised they should go where their hearts led them and not just go where the money is.

Now I do realize that this is not always possible. In some instances when you have a family, you have to make sacrifices for the good of all. You have to consider money and health insurance and a variety of other things. Just being unhappy in a job is sometimes not a good enough reason to change.

Still, I am pleased that I have been able to do what I love, and so far it looks like my boys are able to do so too. Now, I just have to worry that my grandchildren will grow up and be happy in their careers. And I have to make sure they know they are special and can do whatever they want to do.

It must be catching on though. Last week when both grandchildren were visiting us, Walker, the seven-month-old, was crawling around on the floor while his three-year-old sister Genna watched *Cinderella* for the hundredth time.

For some reason, she decided to pay some attention to Walker and got down on the floor so they would be at eye level. 'You know what, Walker?" she asked. "You can be anything you want to be." Walker just looked at her with that wide-eyed admiration he always gives her. Genna continued, "You can even be a baby if you want to."

I guess the message is getting through.

The Story of Bo

You never know what you can do when you put your mind to it. Things that seem like merely dreams do come true if there is enough perseverance and determination. Take for example my nephew Bo Cooper.

Bo has been musical since the day he was born. I can't remember seeing him when he wasn't playing a toy piano or beating on a play drum. It comes naturally to him because my brother is super talented. Always has been. He was the one in our family who could play the piano, clarinet, and organ. My father always said he inherited his musical abilities from my grandmother Cooper who we called "Ma-Ma." She had never received piano lessons but could play by ear.

My brother did take piano lessons and when he was an adult he taught them. He was the one who taught Bo from the earliest age. I always thought it would be hard to teach your own child, but he and Bo seemed to do all right with the lessons. I never heard of any terrible arguments they had over the piano requirements.

Bo became interested in Christian music while he was in college. He made friends with some people who were active in that field and later he and his brother toured with a Christian musical group. Bo played keyboard and his brother Todd played the saxophone. At times, the two of them talked about being a musical duo known as the Coopers. That dream never happened.

Year after year went by with Bo struggling to find that one job that would give him security and a chance at stardom. And in the meantime he put his personal life on hold. There were just so many jobs to audition for, and so many tours to make when he got a job.

He finally moved to Nashville and for a few years toured with Michael W. Smith. This was his closest brush with the big time. After that job ended, he stayed in Nashville working part-time jobs here and there. I thought the dream was finally over for him. But then my brother told me he had gotten a "semi-permanent" job with a new group called Rascal Flatts. I didn't know anything about them and had never heard their music. I just knew they were basically a country group.

Well, Rascal Flatts has become one of the biggest groups in country music today. Bo, who now calls himself "Boh" Cooper, is not one of the lead three guys, but he is part of the backup band that tours with them. I was watching Country Music Television (CMT) the other night and there they were on the Top 10 Countdown. It was some song about love and breakups and it all took place in the rain. Go figure!

Anyway, the fascinating thing was seeing Bo playing keyboard and singing his heart out. It looks like he has achieved his dream. He is making a living playing his music and singing some songs.

And the icing on the cake? Well, he's also fallen in love. At age thirty-nine, he has finally met the right girl at the right time. She works with Brooks and Dunn in the public relations field, so she is very familiar with the business. They have that in common as well as a shared faith. The marriage is scheduled for May 4.

All those years of struggle have finally paid off. It didn't come easy, but it did arrive. Dreams do come true. Some just take longer than others.

Senior Sounds So Old

This growing old thing is certainly complex. On one hand, I feel just as young as I ever did, while on the other hand I look in the mirror and see my father. Now when did that happen!

I remember one day when I was a teenager talking with my friend Agnes about life. We did that a lot. Anyway, during this session of very important talking we discussed age. At the time my father was forty-six years old and that seemed ancient to sixteen-year-old me. I asked Agnes what she thought it would be like to be that age. Agnes, who was a wise seventeen-year-old, said it was probably just constantly depressing. I agreed it probably was.

I think somehow Agnes and I thought we would be young forever. Well, believe me, you don't stay young forever. Those days and years pass with rapid speed the older you get. Still I have liked every age I have been. I like being middle aged and I liked being young. I hope I like being old.

A few days ago, I was interviewing a film director and age came up in the conversation. I asked him if he could stay one age forever what would it be. He responded four years old. He said he had a four-year-old son and every thing about that age seemed wonderful.

I wouldn't want to be four forever. I would want to be of an age that I had some sense and I had a good income. The most inconvenient thing about being young was that people could tell you what to do. Middle age brings a freedom from that.

I know women think about aging differently than men. I talked with a woman the other day and she was upset that people over fifty are somehow lumped into a senior citizen category that contains people who are one hundred. I had to admit she made a valid point. Why do we say that anyone fifty or fifty-five is a "senior"?

It seems particularly unfair to women who look so young these days. They stay in better shape and overall better health. To call them seniors at fifty or fifty-five really isn't fair. I sometimes think "seniors" should be those eighty and older. Still I have to admit I claim that "senior discount" at Wendy's every chance I get.

Every time I say "senior discount, please" my wife adds, "It's him, not me." She is much younger than I am and as much as she loves me she doesn't want anyone thinking she is my age.

So come on, America. Let's come up with a new term for those fifty to eighty years of age. How about Mature? That doesn't sound like you are one step away from death but it does signify you aren't a teenager. But make sure you still have a "mature citizen discount" available. I like saving money at Wendy's.

A Life Lesson

I have spent most of my life trying to make my brother Thom see the error of his ways. From early childhood on I have talked, ranted, and argued with him about the best way to live his life. Even though I am the younger brother, I still have tried to impart my wisdom to him. But he doesn't listen. He has never listened!

One of the big things in our relationship has been how he has treated his wife (now ex-wife) and children. To say my brother is frugal is to blow the definition of frugal out of the water. He takes advantage of all the shopper's discounts and uses coupons like they are the only way to go.

I remember once saying I wanted to go eat at a certain fast-food place. He said, no, they didn't give senior discounts. At that time I wasn't entitled to any such discount but even if I had been I would have still wanted to go. He refused to go. I even offered to pay and he still refused to go.

When dealing with his wife and kids he always cautioned them to be cautious with money, and he doled out his funds with great and careful care. His wife was his exact opposite. She would give to any person in need or with a sad story. And with her children she was generous to a fault. I remember over and over hearing stories from their children about how cheap Dad could be and how generous Mom always was.

Whenever I talked with my brother about his stingy ways, he defended them to the fullest. He cited, "Money didn't grow on trees" and "You never know what tomorrow will bring" —all those adages about staving off poverty. I always came back with my favorite saying, "If it's a problem money can fix, it isn't a problem."

A couple of years ago my brother was diagnosed with lymphatic cancer. It scared both of us silly though he remained calmer than I did. I knew he was alarmed but he maintained a brave front. Through the diagnosis, and the radiation and chemotherapy treatments, he never let on how scared he was.

He came through the treatments just fine and all of the checkups have been positive. He has been cancer free for fourteen months now. I am grateful to the core of my being, and so is he.

Last weekend, my wife and I were in St. Petersburg visiting her parents and I went to see my brother. We spent the afternoon talking and one of the subjects was his son Bo's wedding, which was going to be held in Key West. He was telling me that he had to get measured for a tux for the wedding. Knowing how he is, I mentioned he should be prepared for it to be expensive. He said it was no big thing.

Later, he talked about the rehearsal dinner and how he really wanted to do it up great for Bo. He said he had heard about a place in Key West owned by Kelly McGillis (of *Top Gun* fame) that was super nice. I mentioned that it is also supposed to be expensive. He shrugged that off too.

I couldn't stand it. I looked at him and asked, "What happened to you? When did you get so generous?"

He sat there looking happy and healthy and said, "One thing you told me was that if money could solve it, it isn't a problem. I finally understand what you mean."

He didn't say anything else but I understood. The cancer had been a problem; things that cost money weren't. Now that's a simple thing to learn, but sometimes it takes a while.

A cancer survivor once told me her cancer was a gift, an unwanted one but a gift just the same. She said it opened her eyes to the real values of life. I think that is what happened to my brother

Happy birthday, Tommy.

We Thought We Would Be Young Forever

One day when I was ten or eleven years old I remember talking with my friend Agnes. We were talking about how our parents wouldn't let us do something we wanted to do. We decided it was because they were old and just didn't understand kids. In our frustration with my folks I said to her, "I am never getting old." And she replied, as only a ten-year-old can, "We'll always be young!"

I think at that time we actually believed that to be true. We thought we would stay young forever. I mean, who could comprehend getting older? It just didn't seem possible back in those days when a week was ten years long and a month was an eternity. Youth was what we had been blessed with and youth was what we would keep.

In my teenage years, I relished being young. Time was my friend and not my enemy. All of the people I spent time with were young like me. Older people seem to have been born old and stayed that way. In my heart I could hear what Agnes said, "We will always be young!"

Even after I grew up and got married and had kids, I prided myself on being young. I remember hearing my son Sean tell his mother one day, "I want to be young like Dad when I grow up. He knows all the songs and all the names of the movies." Hearing that, I knew I was still young.

It helped too that all my friends still looked young, at least they did to me. They didn't look like people in their late thirties or early forties should look. Back when I was a kid people of that age looked ancient. They moved like old people; they looked like old people; they smelled like old people.

Lately, however, when I look in the mirror, I see someone who looks like he is past his prime. What hair I have left is turning gray, and when I exhale my stomach seems to paunch out further than it should. I was rubbing my face the other day and my wife told me to quit doing that. "Why?" I asked.

"Because gravity will pull your skin loose without you having to help it," she answered. "You need to tighten your face, not loosen it." As she said that I looked in the mirror and it did seem my face was sliding south. My dimples had become indentations, and my smile lines were now just wrinkles. Gravity was at work.

Still inside I knew I was still young. I knew that I could still run and jump if I wanted to. I just didn't want to. I could keep up on any subject and show I had a great sense of humor. There was nothing inside me that wasn't modern and up to date.

That is what keeps us going. Others may age, but we don't. I remember my friend Norene Jones. She was the babysitter for our children when she was in her late seventies. When we would have conversations she would sometimes talk about the old people she knew. She talked about "them" like they were another species. She didn't fit in that group and she would tell you that quickly.

My stepmother does the same thing. She is eighty-six and she still talks about some old people at her church. She is still young; they are old. And I understand. Each of us as an individual sees our self still young—inside. In that way we fulfill what my friend Agnes said so many years ago. We will stay young forever!

No More Peeps from Those Chicks

Freedom of speech is a wonderful thing. I am so glad we have it in this country, especially when we hear about how you can literally be murdered in other countries for speaking your mind. So when I hear people speak out, whether I agree with them or not, I applaud their right to do so.

Which brings me to the "Chicks." The Dixie Chicks are three young women who have accumulated a lot of wealth and fame by creating country western music. They have bordered on controversy a few times and went into overdrive with "Earl Had to Go," which was a song about justifiable homicide. It was a song Velma Kelly and Roxie Hart of *Chicago* fame would appreciate and understand.

Recently the Chicks took their political views out of the songwriting arena and into the spoken-word arena. On their recent tour of Europe while they were performing in England, Natalie Maines, the non-sister "chick," stepped forward to say that the Dixie Chicks are from Texas and they are ashamed that President Bush is from there too.

Well, this started a firestorm of anti-Chicks fervor. People were smashing their Chicks CDs or having parties to burn their albums. It got so bad that Natalie issued a statement saying she was sorry she was disrespectful to the office of the president. For a lot of people, that was too little too late. Radio stations still banned their music.

The two people I want to hear from are Emily Robinson and Martie MaGuire. They are the two sisters who formed the Dixie Chicks in the first place. Natalie Maines was a late invitée to the party, though many credit her with the huge success the Chicks have had. Still, it was the "outsider" who opened her mouth and caused the trouble. So I think it is more than time that we heard from the sisters and how they feel about it all.

As for me, I do say that Natalie had the right to speak her mind. And I also think people have the right to disagree with her and not buy her CDs any more. Freedom plays both ways. I also want to add that I wish if people are going to say something controversial, and especially something negative about our country and our political system, then they should do it within our country. Don't wait until they go overseas and then say it. That to me is the height of poor taste.

So Martie and Emily, let's hear from you. But when you get ready to say it, say it in the good old USA.

A Fantastic Festival

This past weekend Jackie White and I manned a booth at the Mulberry Street Arts and Crafts Festival in Macon. Jackie is the accomplished author of such books as *Whisper to the Black Candle* and *The Empty Nursery*. As part of the Cherry Blossom Festival, she and I sold and signed books last Saturday and Sunday.

I can't remember when I have had such a good time. It wasn't just the selling and signing of books, it was getting to see the city of Macon in bloom, and also getting to meet and greet some of the nicest people I have ever met. Everyone was friendly. Everyone was having a good time. Everything was just perfect. God was in heaven and all was right with the world. Well, it was right with my little corner of the world.

Two women came in and talked with us. They were American Indians who make their home in Portland, Oregon. The oldest told us that she and her two children had come with her friend on a tour, which included a stopover at the Cherry Blossom Festival. She said she had no idea Georgia and particularly Macon was so beautiful. She also commented on how friendly everyone was.

She added that her children wanted to stay there and not go home. The fact that people spoke to them, smiled at them, and told them how happy they were to see them, it all had made them want to live in this part of the country.

I think those of us who live here tend to overlook just how special our part of the world is. It's beautiful, it's friendly, and it's special. When I was in college there was a girl in my class named Sandra. She was someone I had known for a long, long time. She was pretty. We all knew that. But we didn't think she was extra special. Then one day a photographer came to the campus and asked her to model for some pictures he was going to take.

When the pictures were printed we were all amazed. Sandra was gorgeous! And the next time we saw her we realized she had always been gorgeous. We were just so used to her being around that we didn't recognize her amazing beauty. That's the way it is with us and our area of the state.

On a different note, a woman came into our tent and bought some books. She told us about the strange times that she, a Georgia native, was having teaching school in Ohio. She said she had had to teach her fourth graders to say "Yes, ma'am" and "No ma'am" as well as "Thank you" and "Please."

One story she told concerned her students and a test they were taking. In her instructions before the test she told them to "put up their pencils when they were finished." While they took the test, she graded some of their other work. When the test time was up, she looked up and saw most of her students sitting at their desks with their hands raised, holding their pencils. They had put them "up" when they were finished.

I love that story. I loved my time at Cherry Blossom this year. I loved that these people had a great weekend too!

Walker Is My Main Man

Over the past few years I have written a lot about my granddaughter, Genna Ray Cooper. Since she is the daughter I always wanted to have, but didn't, I tend to think everything she says or does is just the cutest and most wonderful thing possible. But there is another baby in my son Sean's household. His name is Walker Levi Cooper.

Walker is one year old, and one of the most beautiful babies you have ever seen. I am sure the Gerber people are going to be calling any day now to ask him to be on the labels of their baby food jars. He has a head full of dark brown hair and the biggest, bluest eyes since Paul Newman was a baby.

What is most outstanding about Walker is his demeanor. Whereas Genna rushes to meet the day, every day; Walker is laid back to the extreme. He doesn't walk, he ambles. And he does it very nicely too. If you are visiting him, he will amble over to where you are and just stand there looking at you. Maybe, if you are lucky, he will give you a kiss. He tends to do that because my man Walker wants everyone to be happy.

He especially wants Genna to be happy. Every once in a while he ambles into her field of vision. She will swoop down on him and give him a big squeeze. He usually endures this with a look of pure love on his face. He completely loves his sister and basks in her attention, but sometimes her squeezes get a little too tight. (Genna is a proponent of tough love.) When this happens he will give a little wail that brings his momma running.

Although he is walking—make that ambling—now, he still enjoys just sitting in his high chair playing with a single toy. It usually just needs to be something that makes a sound or rolls. If you want to see him in pure delight, give him something that rolls and makes noise. The best thing about this is that he can entertain himself for long periods of time. He really doesn't want to be a bother to anyone.

It is amazing to me to me how different children can be. Genna is my redheaded dervish girl. She embraces life and makes it a wonderful game, a game that she plays every day and on her terms. Walker is the epitome of cool. I have never particularly liked that term, but there is just no other way of describing him.

He is laid back, peaceful and content. He is my main man Walker, the coolest dude I know.

Traditions

Several years ago I first saw the play *Fiddler on the Roof*. Later I saw the movie, and a few more renditions of the play. In other words, I know this show pretty well. For those of you who don't know it, it concerns a man named Tevye who lives in Russia. He has three daughters and he is constantly trying to remind them of the traditions of his family.

There is an actual song in the play called "Tradition" and most of the actors who play Tevye sing this one song with gusto and enthusiasm. I often thought I would like to audition for the chance to play the role of Tevye because I like that song and what it says so much. But then I would also think that I don't have any real acting talent and I would let that dream slip away.

But still I do hold on to the thought that traditions are valuable for any family. There are two that I really maintain as being inviolate. One is being together with my friends and family on Christmas night. My wife and I, and our sons, have been getting together with three or four other couples on Christmas night for years and years now. It is a gathering at the same place with the same friends and I love it. It's *tradition*.

We also get together at another friend's house on Easter Sunday afternoon. Again, it is a time for friends and family. We all eat dinner together and share fun and friendship for a full afternoon. I love it. It's *tradition*.

Those are the two times I ask that my boys come home and take part in the celebrations. I can take skipped birthdays. I can take missed anniversaries. But Christmas night and Easter afternoon, those are the times I want my family with me. It's *tradition*.

A few days ago, I learned that my son Sean isn't coming home with his wife and children for Easter. He isn't coming. His wife isn't coming. My grandchildren aren't coming! He has some insufficient excuse about having to be at church in Moultrie where he is a youth minister. So? He also said that it would be hard to get here for lunch when it is an almost two-hour drive from Moultrie. Again I ask, "So?"

Then he added that he would have to be back for services that night. So? And also that it was hard to make that quick a trip with the kids being only three and one year old. So? I mean I couldn't believe he couldn't even come up with a decent excuse. All I could do was keep saying to him "It's Easter! It's *tradition*."

So this Easter Sunday Sean and his family will go to his church, will eat an Easter dinner at his house, hunt eggs with his kids, and not take part in our traditional gathering. That's the way the breakdown of our society starts, I guess, with kids going off and doing their own thing and starting their own traditions (notice the lack of emphasis).

I can sense the presence of Tevye standing beside me as I bemoan my fate. He understands my pain. Wait, I feel a song coming on. It's a duet, and it is—"*Tradition*"!

Patrick and Melissa—A Love Story

When I was in college one of the prettiest girls in my class was named Melissa. She was pretty, popular, and nice. She had her choice of boyfriends and dated a variety of people. But one of the people she hung around most with was one of our professors named Dr. Patrick Burns.

Patrick was not handsome in any sense of the word. He had spiky hair, eyes too large for his face, and he sweated all the time. He had the appearance of an unmade bed. But for some reason Melissa liked him. Her friends teased her regularly about Patrick and she always just brushed them off by saying he was just a friend.

I would see Melissa and Patrick on campus from time to time walking between classes. There never seemed to be anything romantic between them and I accepted the strange fact that they were friends.

Then tragedy struck. Melissa began to have problems with her coordination. She actually fell down a few times as she was rushing to various classes. She went to her doctor who referred her to a specialist. After having many tests, she was diagnosed with a severe muscular disease. I never knew specifically what it was, but I knew it could be fatal in some cases.

Melissa accepted her illness but she also wanted to finish college while she could. She loaded up with courses and worked her head off to get a full four-year course done in as little time as possible. Patrick was the one who advised her and guided her and helped with her studies. I would see them walking now and he held her arm to steady her as she moved about the campus.

Her condition deteriorated quickly. Soon she was in a wheelchair and her vision began to fail. But Patrick was still by her side. I don't know if it was her condition or just the feeling that life could end at any time, but word soon spread that Melissa and Patrick were getting married.

Nobody questioned why Melissa was marrying Patrick. A few did question why he was marrying her. But when you saw the way he looked at her with so much total devotion, you knew.

When I graduated from college, Melissa and Patrick were still together. She depended on him for everything and he gave his all to her with total happiness in doing so. I never saw a couple so much in love. I never saw two people any happier.

Melissa died two years after I graduated from college. Patrick was at her side. I haven't seen him much since her death, but the few times I have he told me that he is happy. He says he has his memories and that is enough, and I think that is true.

I think back to how my friends and I used to tease Melissa about Patrick. We just couldn't see any reason for her to hang around him. But Melissa knew. She saw the heart that beat with love for her, and the spirit that would protect her all her life.

Sometimes love is blind. Sometimes love is all seeing. Sometimes we are fortunate to witness a true love story.

Idol Chatter

Years ago I used to review plays. I covered plays in Perry; I covered plays in Warner Robins; I covered plays in Macon. I could see as many as three plays in a week, and loved every minute of it. In truth, as much as I love movies there is nothing like the excitement of a live play performed by a good cast.

With my coverage of movies expanding and the reviewing of videos added to my projects, something had to go. And what went was my reviewing of plays. I still love them but I don't go to see each one these days.

To feed my hunger for live performing I have taken to watching *American Idol*. I am addicted to the show and have watched this year since they had the first auditions. Some of the kids on the show have been awful but others have been amazing. I found myself asking, "Where do they find talented kids like this?"

A few nights ago, I went to a performance of *Footloose* at the Westfield School in Perry. I was impressed with the kids in lead roles, kids such as Kate Green, Blair Sexton, Patrick Coussens, Dorothy Dannenberg, and Michael Walker. They all sang, acted, and danced with enthusiasm and energy.

But it was Phil Hebert's performance as Ren McCormack, the Kevin Bacon role in the movie of the same name that really blew me away. This young man took control of the stage as soon as he walked onto it. He was a natural in the role and seemed to be completely at ease as he performed.

I was first impressed with just his presence on stage. He seemed at home there. Then he began to sing and I was pleased with the way he sounded. A few minutes later he began to dance and I was impressed with his natural rhythm. Then he did an amazing back flip across the stage.

When the play was over, I was proud of each and every one of the students who had performed during the course of the night. They gave the audience two solid hours of enjoyment. And then there was Phil Hebert. He would have gotten rave reviews from Randy, Paula, and Simon (for those not in the know, those are the three *American Idol* judges).

When they start auditions in Atlanta this fall for the next *American Idol*, Phil Hebert ought to go up and give it a try. He has the looks, the talent, and the personality to go all the way. Kelly Clarkson has nothing on him (She won the first *American Idol*.).

You watch these super-talented kids who are trying to make it in show business and you wonder where they came from and how they got so polished. Well, the answer is in high schools across America. There they are getting a chance to sing, dance and act in plays that are no longer amateur-night events. These are polished performances that should make us all proud.

Watching Phil Hebert in *Footloose* made me think back to the first time I saw Bobbie Eakes in the Warner Robins High School "Follies." She took her talent and made it in Hollywood. I think Phil could, too.

Going Home

A few days ago I arrived home and found several messages on my answering machine. One of them was from Stewart MacPherson. Stewart is the manager of Henderson Village, the rustic resort located near Perry. His message was brief and stated he wanted to catch up on what was going on and asked me to call.

I immediately knew why Stewart wanted me to call. He wanted to tell me he was leaving our area and going back to Scotland, where he was born and raised. When I got him on the phone, I told him as much, and he laughingly acknowledged that I was right. "How did you know?" he asked. "Who told you?"

I reminded him that when I had interviewed him for *H Magazine* a couple of months ago he told me he was at Henderson Village on a four-year plan. He said he had told Bernard Schneider, the owner of Henderson Village, that he usually only stayed at one place for four years. By this time he felt his work was done and he was ready to move on to something else.

He had also told me he wanted to eventually move back to Scotland. That's where he and his wife want to raise their two girls, and that is where his own heart has stayed. There's something about these Scotsmen; they can no more get Scotland out of their blood than a Southerner can forget the South.

I wasn't surprised that Stewart was leaving. What did surprise me was that he had bought a castle/hotel in Scotland. I later saw a picture of the place and it is massive and truly impressive.

It also surprised me that Stewart says he is leaving on June 3. That's quick, but I guess when you're ready to go, you're ready to go. Plus, he has already handpicked his successor, a gentleman from the Orlando area and Stewart says he will do a great job at Henderson Village. Maybe so, but he has some awfully big shoes to fill.

In the past few months, Stewart has had me out to Henderson Village to do a "one-man show" for some guests and tour groups. We had talked about doing some more this fall. I reminded him when we talked that I hoped the people in Scotland would understand my "Southern humor" when I came over there to do a show at his new hotel. When he didn't immediately respond, I prodded him with the fact I had always wanted to see Scotland and that my wife had relatives there.

He then responded in some obscure way saying, "We would have to talk about that." It sounded something like "the check is in the mail." In other words, I'm not going to pack my bags just yet.

Stewart has been an integral part of our community since he arrived here four years ago. He has welcomed two babies into his family, and lost one dog. His beloved Angus, who was the mascot of Henderson Village, died earlier this year. Stewart and his family really loved that dog, so I know a part of their hearts will always be here with his memory.

Change is hard for me—any change. I like for my friends to stay right where they are and never pack up and move away. I don't even want them moving to Macon or Warner Robins. And Scotland, well, that is forever away.

Still, I know that Stewart wanted to go home. Its not that he didn't like our area and all of us, he just wants to be back on his own land in his own country. Maybe some day our paths will cross again, but till then I can only say "Godspeed and God Bless!"

Dreaming like a Rich Man

I mentioned that I have always identified with Tevye, the father figure in *Fiddler on the Roof*. I have always liked the song he sang titled "Tradition." Well right now I am thinking of another Tevye song. The one called "If I Were a Rich Man."

What brought it to mind was something my wife said this weekend, and her sister coming up for her fiftieth birthday. My wife Terry made them appointments at a day spa in Macon to have facials, pedicures, manicures, etc. When they returned home, I asked my wife how it had been. "If I were rich, I would do it every week," she said enthusiastically.

After she said that, in my mind I kept asking myself what would I do if I were rich. And I mean Lotto-winning, *Who Wants to Be a Millionaire*-playing rich! I began by thinking about the things I wouldn't want. I wouldn't want a boat. I have never wanted one. I don't have any desire to haul a boat to the lake or wherever and then spend the day riding around on the water. Nope, I don't want a boat.

Wouldn't want a swimming pool. I like to swim, but I wouldn't want to have to worry about the upkeep of the pool. And I sure wouldn't want to worry about the neighborhood kids falling in and drowning. And even if I hired somebody to take care of it, I would still worry if it were being done right. Nope, wouldn't want a swimming pool.

Wouldn't want a new car. I love the car I've got. It suits me perfectly. I trust it to get me anywhere I want to go. It is a car with a calm personality and its seat fits my back. Plus, its heater is just the right degree of hot, and its air conditioner gets it just cool enough. Nope, I wouldn't want a new car.

Wouldn't want a new house. I can't imagine living anywhere else but where I do. I know my house so well that I can walk through it at night in the dark and never have to turn on a light. I know where every table, chair, and anything else is. Get a new house? Don't be crazy. Nope, I don't want a new house.

I guess I could give the money to my kids or put it in trust for my grandkids, but then they would never have the thrill of wanting something for a long, long time and finally saving enough money to buy it. The things Terry and I have gotten after waiting have been the best things of all. I wouldn't want my children to miss out on that.

So, I guess I would just put the money in the bank and draw out a few dollars from time to time and use it for essentials. As for the rest of the time, well, I have enough to be comfortable; and better than that, I am comfortable with what I've got.

Tevye may have wondered what it would be like to be a rich man, and in the play he would have definitely opted for the money. But as for me, well I am doing just fine. I may not be wealthy but I am content. From my vantage point that is the greatest treasure of all.

Habitually Late

When my boys were growing up I could never go to bed until they were in the house at night. As they got older, this meant my staying up later and later. Still, it was worth a little less sleep in order to know they were safe and sound.

Once they left home and went off to college, I got a good night's sleep every night—except when they came home. Then it was stay-up time again. This pattern remained until they were out of college and off on their own. And now that they are twenty-eight and thirty I thought my "stay-up time" was behind me. It isn't.

Recently JJ, my oldest, told us he was coming home in order to attend a wedding in Macon. He would leave his Durham home around five in the afternoon and be at our house around midnight. My other son Sean and his wife and kids were also coming to our house that night. This meant that the brothers would get to see each other and JJ would get to see his niece and nephew.

About seven o'clock on Thursday night, I got a call from JJ. He had run into a hailstorm outside of Charlotte. There had been no overpasses to hide under and his car had gotten pelted pretty good. He said it sounded like the hailstones were going to crash through the car windows. He was not a happy camper. His car is fairly new and he has kept it in good shape. Now, it was pockmarked by hailstones.

The storm had also slowed him down and so he would be late. After getting something to eat, he would be home by 1:00 A.M.

Sean and his family got in around ten. The kids were already asleep when they brought them in from their car. My wife, Terry, visited with Sean and Paula for a while and then went to bed. I stayed up. I had a feeling JJ would call again. He did.

It was after midnight when I got his next call. He had made it through Atlanta but was now stuck in traffic on the other side. He said there was road construction ahead and he was not moving at all. We talked about alternate routes if and when he could ever get to an exit, but he was really not a happy camper now.

The next call I got, well, it was after one and he had gone maybe two miles. He now estimated his arrival time to be around three in the morning. Sean and Paula now decided they would go on to bed. I couldn't, even though JJ had specifically told me not to wait up.

He finally walked in the door at twenty-five minutes to three. His first words were "What are you doing up?" But you know what, he looked happy to see me. We spent a few minutes talking about his journey and then I went to bed.

I was exhausted the next day, but I didn't care. I could no more have gone to bed with him on the road than fly to the moon. I just had to know he was safely home before I could even think about getting to sleep.

Some habits die hard and some never do. I was sleepy while I was saying my prayers that night, but I was also calm as I thanked God for giving my son a safe journey home.

Cowboys Make the Best Heroes

For kids who were born before the 1950s there always seemed to be an abundance of heroes. There were noble politicians, revered ministers, supreme athletes, and of course cowboys. There was even a song written about the fact that "My Heroes Have Always Been Cowboys." Yes, as long as John Wayne was alive and kicking, kids had someone to look up to who seemingly wouldn't let them down.

But what about today? We pick up the paper and read about John F. Kennedy's newly revealed sexual escapade. We find out that one more intern and one more politician had a fling. And all of this was when Kennedy was president and we were all supposedly living in Camelot. Poor Guinevere (Jackie-O)...he certainly made a fool of her.

Then there is Bill Bennett. He wrote a book called *The Book of Virtues*. Plus, he made his career as a talking head on television arguing about the wrongdoing of Bill Clinton. Now we find out he had a weakness for gambling—a big weakness.

Then there are the athletes. It is just commonplace to read about a ballplayer of some sort going into rehab one more time. Or even worse being charged with some criminal assault or other horrendous action. Some of those baseball cards might as well be wanted posters.

So who is left? Clergy? Well, have you read the stories about the Catholic priests? The Catholic Church really took a hit on that one. But the Protestants are not home free either. We've had out share of scandals that have burned up the presses. Clay feet are clay feet in any denomination.

So what are the kids of today supposed to do? Where are the cowboys they are supposed to emulate? I honestly don't know the answer. I wish I did. But between the natural ability of men and women to be less than perfect, and the desire of the media to hold it all up to the light of day, heroes don't have a chance.

Nobody's perfect. Maybe that's what we had better stress to our kids. Some are closer to perfect than others, but no one lives and doesn't make a mistake. So maybe if they want to have someone to look up to, it had better be themselves because they can control their own actions where they can't control those of anyone else.

Inside each of us there is good. I really believe that is true. What we have to do is encourage it in ourselves and in our children. If they recognize the good within themselves, they can hold on to that when the world seems to be going crazy. They need to look for the cowboy inside and let it ride free. The cowboy who stands for justice, tolerance, and fair play.

Roy Rogers, Gene Autry, the Lone Ranger, and John Wayne always were on the side of right. We need to look at ourselves and make sure we are on that side too. Maybe a little cowboy spirit in 2003 would give our kids a chance to have some heroes once again. It would be a shame if they couldn't.

Tomato Juice and Cheese Crackers

Nobody cooks any more. Have you noticed that? People still eat, but they eat out. I was reminded of this when I went to Florida this past weekend. It was my father-in-law's eightieth birthday and we were helping give a party for him. We stayed with my sister-in-law, who is a wonderful person. She just isn't a cook.

I actually thought about smuggling in food for the duration but decided against it because of a previous experience. My wife Terry and I were visiting some old friends in North Carolina, Marty and Mary. Mary was notorious for not knowing what a kitchen looked like, but she and Marty were on a first name basis with every take-out place in Winston-Salem.

Knowing that our friends were non-cookers and sporadic eaters, I convinced my wife we should take a cooler and some crackers. I included in the cooler Diet Cokes and tomato juice. I took ten packs of cheese and peanut butter crackers that I thought would tide me over during the hunger sessions that were sure to come. We were only staying three days so I thought I had it made.

Marty and Mary have three kids, so I swore my wife to secrecy about the drinks and crackers. I knew if the kids found out, they would swoop down like a horde of locusts and munch and drink till everything was gone. Marty and Mary didn't keep drinks and crackers on hand so these kids were deprived.

We were staying in their daughter's room and it was at the end of the house. The night we got there I quickly declined Marty's offer to help carry in our bags. I managed to get all the bags and the cooler in without being noticed. Then I laid clothes over the cooler to camouflage it. That night before I went to bed I had a Coke and a pack of crackers.

The next day we ate out a couple of times, but when it got to be bedtime I was hungry again. Terry, my wife, was still sitting up talking with Mary when I went to our room. I decided tomato juice and crackers were called for. I opened the cooler and pulled out a can of tomato juice. When I popped the top, tomato juice sprayed everywhere. It went on me, but primarily it went on the curtains in our room.

I was horrified! It looked like a mad slasher had gone on a rampage in the room. I anxiously looked around to see what I could use to clean it up. I was afraid to use a guest towel as I thought I would stain it. So I used the white shirt I had been wearing. I went into the bathroom and got it wet and started scrubbing those curtains like mad. Miraculously, the stains came out. I think God worked a miracle because I was praying so hard for Him to do something.

I stuffed the shirt in our bag and got into bed. The next night Terry asked if I was going to have some juice and crackers. I told her no. I said I had decided it was not nice to sneak food in someone's home. She agreed and to my knowledge never noticed the slightly damp curtains.

I still think the idea of the drinks and crackers was a good one. It was just the execution that got screwed up. Who knew that tomato juice could fizz like a coke? Not me. Now I just suffer the hunger pangs and keep the room neat where I am visiting. I've always needed to lose a few pounds anyway.

The Female Parson

In the film *The Music Man*, the young boy played by Ron Howard sings a song about the Wells Fargo Wagon coming to town. As he sings, a crowd of townspeople gather around him and look down the street in anticipation of a wagon full of surprises coming round the bend. It is the most exciting thing that has ever happened in their town and they are all going to see it or bust!

I get that same feeling of anticipation as the day approaches for the new minister at the Methodist church to arrive. People would like to be lined up on the street as the car arrives and the new preacher steps out, since she is the first female senior minister that church has ever had.

The anticipation has been building for months, ever since the Bishop announced his appointments of new ministers at various churches. The First Methodist Church of Perry had known they would be getting a new preacher, but they sure didn't know she would be a woman.

Word swept through the town like wildfire. The question on everybody's lips was "what do you think she will be like?" And my Baptist, Presbyterian, and Catholic friends asked furtively, "Are you really getting a woman preacher?" The answer is yes, we are, big deal, let it rest!

When I told my stepmother we were getting a female preacher, she responded, "Really?" Then this staunch Baptist added, "I don't think I could adjust to a female preacher. I just wouldn't want to hear a woman's voice week after week. That would get on my nerves." I wanted to remind her she had had a preacher for years who spoke in a monotone, and that didn't seem to bother her. But respectful person that I am, I just replied, "Well, I don't think that will bother me."

It truly amazes me that so many people think this is a major event. I mean, this is 2003, not 1903. Women have gotten the vote, have joined men in all areas of the workplace, and are hopefully thought of as equals to men in all areas of life.

But this is new. A woman in the pulpit of the First Methodist Church of Perry just wasn't expected, and she might be someone some people won't like. As a matter of fact, she can probably count on that. I have learned over the years that nobody pleases everybody.

There is also a chance she may not please me. I am picky about my preachers. But if I don't like her it won't be because she is a woman. It will be because I don't like her sermons or her ways as a pastor.

I'm keeping an open mind. I won't make a final decision on her for at least four or five weeks. And if you want to see what all the fuss is about, come on down to services this Sunday. But come early as I am sure there will be a crowd!

Weight a Minute

The other day I went to the TV station to tape a movie review. I usually put on my shirt, tie, and jacket after I get there so I can appear fresh on camera. On this day when I finished putting on my shirt and tie, and reached for my jacket I found it was too small for me. The stupid thing wouldn't close in front even after I tugged and pulled with gusto.

I hastily explained to the crew that I must have picked up an old jacket and brought it instead of the one I usually wear. And in truth I honestly did believe that was what had happened. It was only after I got home and couldn't find another jacket anywhere like the one I had on, that it dawned on me. I had outgrown the coat.

Now, my wife has been giving me subtle and not-so-subtle hints lately that I am tacking on some excess pounds. Up till this incident I was able to convince myself she was wrong. When I looked in the mirror I still looked slim and trim. Well, not as slim and trim as I used to, but still slim and trim.

I really don't know what I am going to do to take off some pounds. I know I could diet, but I hate to diet. I like food! I take that back—I love food! Plus I am a creature of habit. Just about every day I head for Wendy's to have my lunch. I get a large chili, large fries, and a large diet coke. I love that food. It gives me comfort. It gives me consistency. And I guess it gives me a few more inches tacked on my waist.

I know I could exercise, but who in their right mind likes to exercise? My wife asked me to go walking with her the other morning, but the thought of dragging all of me around a mile or more of sidewalk gave me the shivers. I just couldn't do it. Still, tomorrow I may walk down the driveway and back. I mean, you have to start somewhere.

All of this is my father's fault. The Coopers are all stocky. We start out pretty slim and then one day you add water and we expand. It is called the Curse of the Coopers and it's been around for ages. My cousin Bill thought he had escaped it. He stayed slim until he was forty-nine. I mean, he only weighed about 165 or 170. Then one day he drank a milkshake and the next morning he was 235. And he never has gotten that weight off.

Worse yet was my cousin Dianne. She was the family beauty and could sing like an angel. We all thought she would make it big in Hollywood, but all she did was make it big. One day, she was a svelte charmer and the next she was full-figured girl, if you know what I mean.

A few years back, I gained a few pounds. I was concerned so I asked my doctor what to do. He gave me some pills that cut my appetite. I mean I didn't want to eat anything. I dropped weight like you wouldn't believe. I also started moving at warp speed. It was driving everyone crazy. So I stopped the pills. The weight came back and brought along some friends.

You know, even thinking about all this is getting depressing. I think I'll just buy a new jacket in a bigger size. That solves my problem and doesn't take any effort at all.

Chasing a Bargain

Deep inside me I know that there is no free lunch. There is no pot of gold at the end of the rainbow; and there is no $200 when you pass "Go." I know these things, but hope still springs eternal that one day I will get something for nothing.

I think all of us want that, but when you are a little bit tight, stingy, or careful with money you want it more. You search for the bargain, you think about winning the lottery, and you always know some long lost relative is going to die and leave you money.

With this kind of attitude you are a sucker for the "fool's bargain." This is the type of bargain that's like fool's gold. It looks like the real thing, but it isn't worth doodle.

Recently, I once again fell for a fool's bargain. It happened when I was talked into accompanying my wife on a shopping trip for our two grandchildren. Now I don't like to shop—at any time. But I do love my grandkids, so I can be harassed into doing it. On this day, my wife had applied the proper amount of harassment and I had succumbed to the pressure.

We ended up in a very nice store where they had some very nice clothes and toys. My wife shopped around and found some things she wanted. She took them to the checkout counter where her total came to forty-six dollars. But then the clerk told us about the "bargain bucks."

"If you spend four more dollars, you will have spent fifty dollars and that will entitle you to a twenty-five-dollar coupon," the clerk said with a smile.

That's all it took. Back to the racks we went and came up with some more goodies for the grandkids. This time our total came to seventy-eight dollars.

"Did we qualify for the bargain bucks?" we asked eagerly.

"Oh, yes," the clerk replied. "and if you spend twenty-two more dollars you will qualify for another twenty-five-dollar bargain bucks coupon."

I guess you can see where this is going. We ended up spending a hundred bucks, but we got two twenty-five-dollar bargain bucks coupons. Clutching them in our hands, we're told the coupons had to be redeemed between June 13 and June 21.

Going home, I felt we had really stumbled on to something good. I mean we had spent a hundred bucks, but we had coupons good for fifty more. I had wandered into good fortune territory.

Time flew by and soon it was June 21. My wife and I hurried to the mall to make our purchases with our "bargain bucks" before they expired. We ended up at the counter with sixty-eight dollars of purchases. My wife stated she had two twenty-five-dollar bargain bucks and would write a check for the remaining eighteen.

This clerk, not the same one we had had before, looked a little bit sheepish and said, "You have to spend fifty dollars in order to use one of your twenty-five-dollar bargain bucks. So you will need to write the check for forty-three dollars."

I was stunned, but she pointed out on the coupon where the small print said just that. My wife could read it, but my trifocals and I could not. Or maybe I was just too overheated to be able to see the fine print.

You won't believe it, but we ended up spending another hundred bucks just to get to use our two coupons. That means we spent two hundred dollars to get a discount of fifty dollars. It was the principal of the thing and the determination to get our bargain.

So never believe in something that sounds too good to be true. Odds are it isn't. Just like a fool and his money, a fool and his "bargain" are soon parted.

The Mediocrity of Movies

Yesterday I went to the movies. Nothing unusual there; I do it all the time. As a general rule, I see two to three movies a week. I also read a book a week, and watch three or four videos as well as two or three TV shows. I am an entertainment critic. It's what I do. And most of the time I love it. But lately I have been in a rut, or the entertainment industry has been in a rut.

It has been months since I saw a really good movie. I mean one where I left the theater feeling truly entertained, enlightened, or informed. Instead I have been subjected to a barrage of "Justin and Kellys," "Alex and Emmas," and on and on and on. Most of these movies have interchangeable actors acting out interchangeable scripts. Where is the magic?

One sore point with me is the language in movies these days. If you aren't a regular moviegoer, you might not know what I am talking about. But if you go as much as I do, then you have been subjected to more profanity and coarse sexual language than you would ever want to hear. Movies now discuss every sexual act known to man in the most graphic ways. And most of the time it is done in an attempt to be funny.

This is also true of TV. I review mostly cable shows from HBO, Showtime, and the like. These non-network programs are as sinfully salty as anything you can see and hear on the big screen. Have you ever watched *The Sopranos* or *Sex in the City*? Well be prepared to be shocked because they lay it all out there in a way meant to get a reaction.

The sad thing is that the nudity, profanity, and violence are being used as substitutes for being smart, witty, or inventive. Now

I like *Friends* even though I know it gets a little raunchy at times. But still it is funny. And I like *NYPD Blue* even though it has nudity, and more and more profanity; but at least it is well acted and interesting.

And how about books? Are Hilary Clinton's memoirs the best the book world can offer? Is the obtuse *The Lovely Bones* a truly good book or just something different? Is it no wonder that Oprah had to go back to John Steinbeck's *East of Eden* in order to have a book to recommend?

I love movies, books, television shows, and the all rest that the world of entertainment has to offer. But something has got to give. I don't want to see us return to a strict world of censorship and bland amusements. Still, I want some sanity to come to light and put things back in the right order and perspective.

The bottom line is I want to be entertained and it is going to take more than a *Charlie's Angels* rehash, or some more *Bad Boys* adventures to take me there. Bring me another *Chicago* or *Identity*, or something even better than those two. There is a lot of talent in New York and Hollywood. I am sure someone knows how to break the mold and make us laugh, cry, or be scared in a truly unique way—a way that doesn't require us to be grossed out while we are watching it.

I will still be seeing the latest movies, books, videos, and television shows, but down deep inside I am hoping for a renaissance. Bring it on! I am ready!

The Best We Ever Had

More than any other season, summertime always makes me think about my South Carolina home. As soon as the weather gets hot, I begin to start reminiscing about "the good ole days." It seems my recollective abilities seem to expand in the heat and I can remember entire conversations that took place when I was growing up.

My father was a bread salesman for most of my youth. Before that, he was a Pepsi-Cola salesman. Now these types of jobs meant he got up early to load his truck and worked late taking the goods around to the various stores. He was always gone in the morning before I woke up and he rarely got home before dark.

His bread truck was not air conditioned; all it had was a little fan that sat on the windshield. Like me, my Daddy was a sweater. The perspiration poured off him in buckets, so this one little fan didn't do much good. Still I never heard him complain—about the heat, about the hours, about life in general.

Daddy got one week's vacation a year. I guess he got other days off like Christmas Day, Thanksgiving, things like that, but he didn't get his birthday off. And to my knowledge he didn't have a set number of sick days. In all the time I lived at home, I never remember him taking a single day off for being sick. Now, that *is* amazing.

I remember hearing him tell my mother one week that he was going to clear one hundred dollars. He worked on a salary plus a commission based on the amount of bread he sold. Whenever he would earn a hundred dollars, we were really in high cotton. Still, you know, I never felt poor. It seemed like we did just about as much with that one hundred dollars as others did with much more.

My family talked about everything. Both my brother and I knew when Daddy made a hundred dollars a week, and we knew when he didn't. There was none of this "Let's keep it from the kids" in our house. We were all a part of the family unit and we all knew the facts of what was facing us. If there was a reason to celebrate we celebrated and if there was a reason to worry, we worried—together.

Saturday was a highlight of our week because we would have a spaghetti dinner. That "dinner" was at noon. The meal at night was supper and it was not as major a meal as was dinner. Anyway, mother cooked spaghetti on Saturday and we would all be waiting for Daddy to come in and eat.

When he did, we would sit down at the table and eat that spaghetti like it was manna from heaven. After it was gone, Daddy would look at my Mother and say, "That was the best spaghetti we ever had." He said that every week. But you know what? He told the truth. Every week that spaghetti dinner was the best we ever had.

When I think back to that house on Holland Street and the times we had there, I don't think a bed ever slept better than the one I had there. I also don't think the air has ever been as fresh as it was there. And I know the food I ate in that house was some of the best food ever cooked.

A few months ago, I was in Florida and my brother Tommy and I went out to eat. We both ordered spaghetti. When we had finished eating, Tommy smiled and said, "That was the best spaghetti I ever had." It wasn't. He knew it and I knew it, but I also knew why he said it. It just stirred something inside us both and saying it was a tribute to our father.

My father died three years ago. He made me promise before he died that I wouldn't forget about him. That is an easy promise to keep. He grows more distinct in my memory with every passing year. He was the best we ever had.

The Man Who Came to
Dinner and Stayed

Sometimes you see things in the movies and you wonder if they could ever happen in real life. You know, like that old movie *The Man Who Came to Dinner*. Could someone actually get stuck with a houseguest and let it go on and on and on?

When my family and I were living in California, we had a houseguest. It was a guy named Donald I had met on a business trip, and he seemed pretty sane and normal. He and I had struck up a friendship at a conference, and so when he said he was coming to California I told him to give me a call and we would have a meal together.

I was living in Redlands and he was coming to LA so I really thought we wouldn't even see each other. Those two cities are about a hundred miles or more apart, and who would drive that far just to have a meal with someone?

A week before Donald was supposed to arrive in LA, he called and said his place to stay had fallen through. He had another place to stay but wondered if he could spend a night with us. Being a good guy, I said yes. A few days later, he called and said the car his relative had told him he could use in LA was in the shop, so could I come down and get him. Dumbly, I said yes again.

He arrived by plane. I went to LA and picked him up and we began his "visit." He came on a Saturday, so we expected him to stay the weekend. He did. And things were doomed from the start. He began by telling us he could only eat certain foods. We went to the grocery store to get some basics and he piled things in the cart he wanted to eat. Being the good hosts, we didn't complain but just paid for everything.

On Monday, he asked if he could use one of our cars. I told him he could take me to work and use mine. My wife, who was working as a teacher, picked me up and brought me home from work. Donald arrived soon after we got home. It was time to eat. He was starved.

The next day he said he was just going to hang around the house so he didn't need a car. When I started to work in mine, I found it was totally out of gas. I barely made it to a service station to fill up.

To make a long tale of misery short, Donald stayed for two weeks, and each day was a little worse than the one before it. He nearly ate us out of house and home; he kept his room (the guestroom) in a mess; and he annoyed my wife and my kids to the extreme.

So why did we put up with it? Well, we were raised to be nice to people. He was a guest in our house and you never are rude to people visiting in your home. Also, we always thought the next day would be the last and we could put up with anything just one more day.

Finally, we took him to the airport and let him out at the check in station. We got his bags out of the car in record time. We patted him on the back, wished him a safe trip, and took off. My boys were screaming with glee, while I let out a sigh of relief. My wife, who never said anything negative in front of the children, threatened me with bodily harm if I ever got us into a mess like that again.

We don't have many overnight guests at my house. When we do, we know when they are coming, and more importantly when they are going. Fool me once, shame on you. Fool me twice, shame on me. And this fool isn't going to be shamed like that again.

My Singing Career

It is funny the twists and turns your life takes. We start out wanting to do or be one thing and end up being something else entirely. When I was a little boy I learned I could make people smile and like me by singing. So I decided I would be a professional singer and have a wonderful career and life. It didn't happen, but for a while I thought it would.

In grammar school, my brother and I entered a few local talent contests and had some success. I particularly remember one time we were in a contest being aired on the radio. My brother Tommy played the piano and sang harmony. I sang lead. The song was "The Wedding Samba." We won the show and collected ten gallons of ice cream.

Later in the sixth grade, I was selected to go to the state vocal competition and sing a solo. I had a very high voice and the song I was singing had a very high note. I did great in rehearsals, but then on the day of competition my voice decided it wanted to change. I cracked that high note from here to kingdom come.

This led to an intermission in my career plans. I had to wait for my voice to change completely before I could make further career moves. Eventually, it settled into a nice tenor range and eventually I began to sing again.

My brother and I developed a pretty solid repertoire of songs. We rehearsed them and rehearsed them and got them down pretty good. He was such a talented pianist that he got a paying job with a small combo. He and this group played a few dances in and around our community. One day my brother told me they needed a singer for a Friday night dance. I was a little nervous about singing in front of a paying crowd, but I figured it was time to get my career as a professional started.

We went to the dance. We sang a few songs. There was a good response. But then the guy who was in charge of the group asked the audience if they had any requests. They shouted out a few song titles and the leader, Jake, said they would play some of them. Jake then turned and asked me if I knew a certain song they had named. I nodded.

The combo started the music and I tried to sing along. I didn't really know the words; I didn't really know the tune. I was awful. I knew I was awful. The crowd knew I was awful. They let me know it by booing. I spent the rest of the night waiting in the car to go home.

I never sang professionally again. The pain and embarrassment were just too much. Rather than becoming more determined, I just gave up that dream on the spot. But I didn't give up singing all together. I still sang at church, and in the shower, and in the car. Basically I sang for my own pleasure—and still do.

I never forgot that awful feeling of being booed. That let me know I didn't have the thick skin necessary for a career in show business. Now, when I watch shows like *American Idol*, I know I made the right choice. Simon would have destroyed me.

Still sometimes when I am riding along in my car singing along with the radio I know I sound good. At least to my ears I do. And in my heart I know that I could have been a contender.

A Family Vacation

Take five adults and two children, put them in a one-bedroom condo for three days and see what happens. That is the experiment my family attempted this last weekend. It wasn't a planned experiment. We weren't being paid for the endeavor. It was just how our end-of-summer vacation ended up.

My wife and I wanted to get the family together at least once during the summer. By the time we talked with my youngest son, Sean, and his family about their availability and then matched their schedule up with my oldest son JJ's, we were down to one weekend that was fast closing in on us.

The boys and I went on the Internet to try to locate a condo with a couple of bedrooms. We found none where we wanted to go. My wife Terry refused to accept this. She started calling around and ended up with a one-bedroom condo at Navarre Beach. It also had two bunk beds in the hallway and a sofa that made into a double bed. She booked it.

That is how I, my wife, my son, his wife, my other son, and our two grandchildren ended up in Florida. We spent three days together and learned what closeness is all about.

We couldn't have survived without my wife's planning. She took toys for the kids and food for the adults. People who eat well are always more cordial, and we ate well. Most of the time we agreed to be at the beach at the same time or at the swimming pool at the same time. But finally on the second day I had to have some time alone. So did JJ.

He and I took off and went to the movies while everyone else went to the mall. I saw a longing look in Sean's eyes as JJ and I pulled out of the parking lot. I knew in his heart of hearts he was wishing he was going to a movie too. Still he is a devoted family man, and his kids needed some time away from the condo.

That night, as JJ and I gave reviews of the movies we had seen (We didn't go to the same one), Sean told us how we had missed out on arcade games and shopping fun. We nicely said we hated we had missed all that—*not!*

It is true that I am a person who needs alone time, and JJ is the same way. It isn't that we are anti-social; we just need some quiet time in our days. Still, he is crazy about his niece and nephew, so he was more sociable than I have ever seen him be. He played games with them, he swam with them in the pool, and he went to the beach. But on the third day, he slipped off again to go to a military museum and to the library.

I have to say that my family did me proud. Each person, even the young ones, did his or her best to be as compatible as possible. There were no arguments of any kind.

But as I write this I am back in my house. My wife is sitting in the den alone and smiling. The house is so quiet you could hear a pin drop. After a long session of family mingling, we are quickly adjusting to it just being us.

There will be other family trips and we will enjoy them. Still, for now the company of two is a wonderful thing.

The Julia Question

The first thing people ask me when I meet them is "What celebrities have you met?" Then before I can get an answer out they ask, "Have you met Tom Cruise?" Or they ask about some other celebrity I have never met. When I quickly reply that I have met Tom Hanks, they usually just mutter something like "Big deal."

Why is it that the people I am asked about are the ones generally that I have never met? I have interviewed a wide range of celebrities from Dolly Parton to Mel Gibson, yet I always get asked about Cameron Diaz or Eminem.

The one star interview that does cause people to open their eyes wide is Julia Roberts. Now, she can set people to talking. I have interviewed her three or four times and she has always been charming and cordial and beautiful. She has also been very accessible and by that I mean that she seems to respond to my questions and not just give stock answers.

Still, I never know what to say when people ask, "What is Julia Roberts really like?" I mean, I don't have a clue as to what she's really like. I know how she seems to be, but I don't have breakfast with her. I don't know her husband. I don't even know her estranged brother Eric.

I do know what I hope she's like. I hope she is a lot like her character of "Shelby" in *Steel Magnolias* without the diabetes problems. That character was so nice and so loving that I would hope Julia couldn't have played her so perfectly without having a lot of the character in her.

There are still celebrities I would like to meet. I would like to meet Elizabeth Taylor. I know she is still alive and so that meeting is still a possibility. The problem is that I want to meet the Liz Taylor of the 1950s and 60s. I want to meet Maggie the Cat from *Cat on a Hot Tin Roof* or Susannah from *Raintree County*. That is the Elizabeth Taylor I still have in my mind's eye. When she was in her prime, she was the most beautiful woman in the world, and I would like to meet that person just one time. Oh well, we all have our dreams.

I would also like to meet Pat Conroy the writer. I have read every book he wrote and just about every article ever written about him. When I first read *The Lords of Discipline*, I knew I had found a kindred spirit. I knew all the emotions he wrote about and most of the places in his locales. We were both the products of a South Carolina educational system and a Southern spirit runs through our veins.

The closest I have come to meeting Pat Conroy was interviewing his wife, who is also a writer. In the world of Six Degrees of Separation, I have a connection. But I want to meet Pat in the flesh. I want to have a long conversation with him about his life, his writings, and his plans for the future.

You know what it all boils down to? I want to know what Pat Conroy is really like.

A Different Side of Celebrity

In this age of instant journalism, we are kept aware of every move and motion of our "celebrities." Most of the time this involves knowing where they appeared drunk or stoned, where they had their romantic trysts, or anywhere that they could be seen in a bad or compromising situation. We seem to like the bad image that titillates and amuses and keeps our interest.

Every once in a while, we learn of the other side of celebrity. That is what this story is about. It is not a story I know first hand. I can only relate it as it was told to me. But it has such resonance and impact, I wanted to share it.

A few weeks ago, country music star Alison Krouse was scheduled to perform in Valdosta, Georgia. She, along with Union Station, was going to put on a show, and fans in the area were waiting for the chance to see her perform. Alison has been a country music favorite for years and each of her shows generally sells out.

One family from Warner Robins was going to the show. A mother packed up her four children in the family van and headed for Valdosta. It was a rainy, rainy day and before the van could safely reach Valdosta there was an accident. The mother died as a result of the crash.

Alison Krauss was told about the accident and on stage she spoke of this lady and each member of her family. Prayers were offered and silence was observed. The show did go on, but with an air of shock and sadness surrounding it.

Later that night, people in the neighborhood where the woman and her family lived were surprised to see a huge tour bus coming on to their streets. Alison Krauss had come to visit the family and offer whatever comfort she could.

I don't know what went on in that house that night. I don't know what words were spoken or what prayers were offered. I did hear that Alison Krauss wrote a letter to the family when she returned home. It seems she had been touched by the woman's death and the knowledge she had gained about the life this fine Christian lady had lived.

Later, during the funeral, a crowd gathered. It seems many people in our community had been touched by her life and affected by her death. The church was packed to overflowing, and in the balcony a woman sat and mourned with the others. She was not dressed in a way to be recognized but rather in a way to play down who she was. Still, many knew that Alison Krauss was there and that she came to offer support and friendship to a terribly grieved family.

We are constantly being bombarded with stories about the dark side of the people in the limelight. We wonder what kind of world we are living in when these are the types of people who are admired. But every once in a while, we hear a story that lets us know that celebrities are people too, just like you and me. They live, they breathe, they are happy, and they grieve.

Alison Krauss had her life touched by a woman she didn't even know. Their spirits connected on a rainy night in Georgia. Who knows the good that can come from that?

Leave Me Alone

It is funny how each person reacts differently to being sick. Now, I'm not talking about major illnesses. I am just speaking of the small things like the flu or a bad cold. Some people want to be hovered over and smothered with attention and care. Others like to be left alone to grump and groan by themselves.

One of my good friends belongs in that first category. Let him feel the least bit bad and he wants his entire household turned into a hospital staff. He wants his wife and kids to rush to his side with books, magazines, and anything else he desires. He also wants a steady supply of hot drinks, hot soups, and all of his "make-you-feel-better" medicines.

I've seen him when he would call for his wife to make a trip upstairs to fluff up his pillows or to get him an extra blanket for the bed. Of course, all of this is constantly prefaced with "Honey, I hate to bother you," or "Honey, if you don't mind." And his tone is one of a man slowly slipping away into a coma—a coma caused by a cold.

When he does get a cold or the flu, he manages to let it hit on a weekend when he is able to stay in bed and be waited upon endlessly. It also means that his wife will be off from her job and able to play nurse to his patient. There is some shrewd planning going on there.

I, on the other hand, am the "leave-me-alone" sick man. When I get to feeling bad, I want to withdraw to my room and be left alone. I don't need or want constant attention. I usually can manage to take all my medicine by myself and can even entertain myself with books or magazines.

When I am feeling bad, I don't want to have to pretend to be Mr. Nice Guy. I want to be able to sulk and stew in my own juices. I can fluff my own pillows. I can get my own extra blanket.

Still I do have to say that the chicken soup my wife prepares is extra special. And just having her in the house when I am ill makes me feel more secure. She does check on me every now and then to make sure I am doing all right.

The great thing about being married for a long time is learning what each spouse needs and wants. My wife is there for me during times of illness, but she doesn't hover. Better yet she doesn't get her feelings hurt because I don't want her to hover.

Some people react to illnesses in different ways. The secret is knowing which type your spouse is and acting accordingly.

Life as the Middle of an Oreo Cookie

My generation has been called the Baby Boomers, but now I think it is time for a new name. We should be called the Oreo Cookies. We are the generation that is stuck squarely in the middle between our parents and our kids, and we provide sustenance to both.

Our parents are the Depression generation. Therefore, they grew up holding on to their money in case another depression came down the road later on. They provided the necessities, but they were not as loose with the gifts and goodies as my generation is. They also were the last generation that had the idea that if you took care of your kids today, they would take care of you tomorrow. And tomorrow has arrived.

Most of my adult life, I repeatedly heard my father say, "Don't ever put me in a nursing home." He was adamant about that. Of course, even after he retired he wouldn't think of moving from his home in South Carolina. I offered repeatedly for him to move to Georgia so I could be closer to him. No way. Wasn't going to happen.

Then, one day, he had to have some surgery. I went up to see him. He told me that I needed to be closer, so I could help look after him. I again made the offer of his moving to Georgia. He looked me straight in the eye and told me he thought I could get a good job in South Carolina—and he meant it. He was the parent, I was the child, and I needed to come home and take care of him even if it meant uprooting my entire family.

I never did move back to South Carolina, and my father never did go into a nursing home. He died at home, which was his fondest wish. But there could have come a time when a nursing home was a necessity, and I shudder to think of the guilt that would have befallen me.

Then there are the children. My generation wants its kids to be happy, happy, happy. And they want it too. Plus they want instant gratification. They want the new house, the new car, the private schools for their kids, the latest in electronic toys—they want it all. And as parents, we rush to try to help them have it.

So on one side, we have the "take care of me's" and on the other we have the "give me's." Do you see why I call us the Oreo Cookie? We are right there in the middle and sometimes it's a tight squeeze.

So why do we try to do it all, and be all for everyone? The answer is two-fold. We do it out of love and guilt. Love is a powerful thing, and guilt? Well, guilt is limitless. It comes in all shapes and sizes and hangs around for a lifetime.

If you are in the forty-to-sixty-year-old age range, welcome to the world of the Oreo. Settle in and get ready to hand out the icing. Everyone will be taking a bite out of you soon.

September Song

September used to be important to me only because it was the month of my birthday and a cause to celebrate. It was also the month that school used to start (way back when I was attending) and marked the end of summer. But in the South we knew that September meant some of the hottest weather was still to come.

That was the image of September I grew up with, and it remained that way for most of my life. But then came September 11, 2001, and September was forever changed. It is now the month of mourning and not just for me, but seemingly everyone.

I have spent the first part of this month looking at "memorial specials" on television. Once again, I have watched the twin towers standing stately in the sky with a bright sun reflecting off their gleaming exteriors. And I have reflected back to where I was and what I was doing on that fateful morning.

I had gotten up early and seen my wife out the door on her way to school. Then I had settled down in front of the TV to see what Matt and Katie had to say. Being hungry, I kept going into the kitchen to see what I could find to eat and because of this I missed the first plane plowing into the building.

When I came back to the TV, they were reporting what had happened and my reaction was that it was a terrible accident. I have never been a fan of flying and it seemed to me that some poor pilot just got messed up with his equipment and hit the building. What seemed to be the most shocking thing about it was how the building seemed just to absorb the plane. It didn't come out the other side; the building didn't topple over; the plane was just taken in and kept there.

Now, I was glued to the TV, so I did see the second plane hit. And in my naïveté I continued to think it was an accident. I actually thought two planes had gotten off course and had hit those buildings accidentally. It wasn't until I heard the reporters talking about the "plot against America" that I began to entertain the thought that it might not have been an accident after all.

Then the real horror began as I learned there were people in those buildings who couldn't be rescued. This again stunned me as I thought with today's technology and scientific advancements this could not be possible. Surely helicopters could land on the roofs or some type of rescue harnesses could be lowered. But they couldn't and that is when people began to jump.

I stopped watching then. I couldn't take the horror. It was only later as I heard the towers were imploding that I stationed myself before the TV. By this time the pictures were focused largely on the people on the ground who were hoping for miracles.

As I rewatched the events of 9/11 play out for me again on the TV memorials, I was struck by how patriotic everyone became in the aftermath. Flags were everywhere and so were signs that said "God Bless America!"

Now two years later the patriotism seems to be waning and it is not politically correct to mention God. For two years now Darryl Worley has been singing a song that asks, "Have you forgotten?" In our hearts we all seem to say, "No!" But maybe we have forgotten how we felt that day. And maybe we have forgotten the reason we waved flags and asked God to help us.

I hope I never see anything again like 9/11. It has turned September into a somber month. At least for those who haven't forgotten.

Payday

A few days ago I was listening to someone giving a talk about 9/11, and they used the phrase "Payday isn't just on Fridays." That phrase struck me and I have been pondering it ever since I heard it.

"Payday" can mean a good or a bad thing. It can mean the receipt of something good such as a paycheck, or an out-of-the-ordinary gift. To me, the best gifts have always been those which come unexpectedly. It's the surprise plus the gift that bring the most joy.

I know if I was ever to win one of those sweepstakes and have Ed McMahon show up at my house I would be overjoyed. Can you imagine just being inside finishing up your noon meal and there is a knock on the door. You open it and there is Ed McMahon with a film crew standing behind him. My luck would be that he would hand me the check and then I would fall over dead from a heart attack caused by the surprise.

I used to go around telling people that I never entered any contests because I never won anything. I just wasn't a lucky person. But then I moved to California for a few years and during that time I was on a quiz show. I won a trip to Greece, a car, various other items and a lot of cash. That ended that story *except* I won them because I answered a lot of questions not because I was lucky!

After I won the prizes, they were sent to me at my home address and they arrived via FedEx or UPS, and I don't think any of them ever came on a Friday. Proving once again that payday, or good fortune, can arrive any day of the week.

But there is another kind of payday. That is the kind where things come due. These events can come at any time and any place, too. Just when you think you might get away with something, payday comes. And usually it comes at a time when you are not prepared to pay it.

When I was small, my brother was forever telling me he was going to tell our parents about something bad I did. He would drag it out forever. I would beg and plead for him not to tell and most of the time he didn't. But sometimes he did.

My mother would send me to my room and tell me to think about my transgression. The whole time I was in there I would be dreading the outcome. I knew there was going to be punishment because my mother didn't play around when it came to misbehavior. And she was smart enough to know that the dread just added to the fear of the punishment.

So I had various paydays for bad behavior and believe me they didn't all come on Friday. They came every day of the week.

We get into ruts some time and think that we only have chicken on Sunday, pizza on Friday night, lawn cutting on Saturday, and payday on Friday. Life, real life that is, isn't like that. Payday isn't always on Friday.

The Villages

Hilary Rodham Clinton once wrote that it takes a village to raise a child. Now, people in Florida are proving it takes a "village" to provide a safe, fun place to retire. At least, that is the way it appeared to me when I went to The Villages, Florida, recently.

The Villages is a retirement community that has virtually become a city. It's located in middle Florida near Wildwood and Leesburg. I went there for a book signing at a wonderful bookstore called the Bookworm. While I was there, I got to explore the area as well as visit with and meet some of the residents.

The majority of the people I met were Northerners who had gotten tired of the winters and had headed South. One couple from Pennsylvania told me they had sworn to each other that they would never, ever move to Florida. But then they had vacationed at The Village and that was it. They sold their home up north and moved in. They haven't looked back.

A very gregarious lady told me she had never lived in a place so friendly. She said that everybody talks to you here, even on the streets downtown as well as in your neighborhood. She said when she lived in New York that you kept your head down and went about your business. You got to where you were going as quickly as possible and didn't really look right or left.

She has decided that in The Village you feel safe so you're willing to let your guard down and have conversations with strangers. She says it's an amazing experience and one that she wouldn't want to change.

A lady standing nearby added that there is a sense of community in the individual neighborhoods. She said her daughters didn't worry about her now since they knew the people in her neighborhood would be watching her and checking on her. "They know if something was to go wrong that the people in the neighborhood would take care of me till they could get down here," she said.

There are about 35,000 people in the Village community now, and there are plans to expand and make room for another 35,000 or more. There are also plans to make more tunnels and overpasses to facilitate the use of the golf carts that the residents use for their basic driving needs. These electronic marvels glide around with little noise and little pollution.

It seems that most of the Village's residents are in the same age range and have the same outlook on life. They are not ready to hang it up and so stay busy with all the activities that are offered. "If there is one complaint to be had about the Village," one man told me, "it's that there is too much to do. You just can't do it all."

The homes in the Village cover a broad range in value. You can go from basic to elaborate. But one thing you can't do is have kids living with you. The Village is a place for adults, senior adults. If you are raising your grandkids, well, this is not the place for you.

I saw more smiles in the Village than I have seen anywhere I have visited lately. People seem to be content and enthusiastic. It seems the Village has taught people that this is not a place to come to while you wait to die. This is a place to come to live!

Dreams Do Come True

About a year and a half ago, I got a phone call from a young woman named Karen. She told me she and I had a mutual friend, and this friend had recommended she call me. The reason for her call was she wanted to work in some area of the entertainment business. Our mutual friend told her I might be able to help.

Something in her voice told me she was sincere in her wishes, and on pure gut instinct I decided to help her— at least as much as I could. I told her about some public relations agencies I knew in Atlanta, and a way to get in touch with them. I also mentioned that some friends of mine were currently making a movie in Atlanta and could use some help. I stressed that they would not be able to pay her, but it might get her foot in the door.

Karen contacted the PR agencies but nothing worked out for her there. Then she contacted my friends who were making a film titled *The Adventures of Ociee Nash*. They were thrilled that she wanted to work for them and invited her up immediately. Karen worked for them for a couple of weeks and they were impressed with her abilities.

Following this film she was hired to help with casting on a film starring Robert Redford and Helen Mirren that was filming in Atlanta. Once again she did a good job and was liked by cast and crew alike. She was bubbling when she called me and told me about meeting Robert Redford.

Karen's next job was with the crew of *Big Fish*, a Tim Burton movie filming in Alabama. Here she got to meet some more stars and also to learn more about casting and production. Things were looking up.

Shortly after she finished working on *Big Fish* she called me and told me she was moving to LA. She asked what I thought and my response was "Go for it!" But secretly I was scared silly for her. LA is a big town and to go out there without a positive job was taking a decided risk. But I gave her the name of a few people I knew and wished her well.

Karen was in LA all of a month before she got her break. She had sent out letters to various studios and production companies. One of the ones she heard back from was Steven Bochco's. He's the man behind *NYPD Blue*. Karen was invited to come in for an interview.

She called me after the interview was over to tell me I might be getting a call as she had listed me as one of her references. I said I would be happy to talk with anyone about her abilities. But in this case I didn't get a chance. They offered her the job the next day without talking to me. She was hired as one of three production assistants for the Bochco Company.

Karen is now happily living and working in LA. She is absolutely exuberant about her job, and she can't quite believe it has all happened so quickly. I remind her that it is certainly not the norm. But Karen has a secret weapon working for her. Its not just the fact that she is smart, and loves the entertainment industry. Her secret weapon is she doesn't mind hard work. That is what made the difference and what guided her to success.

So when you are watching *NYPD Blue* this year stay tuned for the credits. Look for the name Karen Faith Rothwell as a production assistant. That is the name of my friend of whom I am so very, very proud.

Call Me Lucky

A few days ago Linda Johnson died. She was a friend of mine and I really miss her. This is strange because Linda and I were not the kind of friends who saw each other often. We were the type of friends who ran into each other every few weeks or so and were awfully glad to see each other. I would see her at a Book Club meeting or some other social gathering and we would catch each other up on things.

I also know Linda's two daughters, Sandy and Sealy. They are as much fun to be around as Linda was. They always seem to be in a cheerful mood and have a positive attitude. And that was Linda. She was one of the most positive people I ever met. This may seem natural in most people, but with Linda and her crowd it was out of the ordinary. They had enough hardships and problems that they could easily have been bitter and downbeat.

Linda's husband and the girls' father had died young. Linda worked as a teacher to support her family, and she was much loved by all her students. When I met her, she was a widow and a teacher. I could see why her students enjoyed her classes because she was so animated and full of joy.

Because she was so animated, it was a shock when she suddenly became ill and was left paralyzed. I didn't know what had happened to her and I think for a while the doctors were stumped. But then she was finally diagnosed with multiple sclerosis. At that point, they told her she would be paralyzed for the rest of her life.

Once again, I was amazed at her attitude. She still was animated and full of joy. She may have been confined to a wheelchair, but her spirit still had wings. She continued to be a positive influence on anyone who met her. And so were her girls.

The last time I saw her was at a book club meeting. It was close to Easter weekend, and I was the guest speaker that day. Her two daughters were with her and the three of them looked happy as could be.

After I had given my talk and the meeting was over, I went to say hello. We talked for a few minutes and then I told her, "I am so envious of you. Here it is Easter and neither of my boys is coming home to see me. And you have both Sandy and Sealy here with you. It's just not fair!"

She looked at me with a huge smile on her face and said, "You know Jackie, you are right. I am the luckiest woman in the world."

Life doesn't always treat us right. Sometimes things happen that we just don't understand. Linda Johnson had more than her share of hard knocks, but she refused to let them get her down. She knew that the love of family is one of the most important things in life and as long as you have that you are on top.

Because she was surrounded by love, she considered herself the luckiest woman in the world. And you know what? She was right.

Moving into Futureworld

This world is divided into two groups: those who are mechanically inclined and those who are not. I definitely fall into the latter group. I don't know what makes things run, don't want to know, don't care. When I turn the ignition in my car and it runs, that is all I need. What goes on under that hood can remain a mystery forever.

The same is true for all these new mechanical or computer-based gadgets. I just accept them for what they are, too, and never worry about the why. Which is why when my computer goes down, I panic. I have no idea how to get it up and running again. That is why God gave me two sons who do know about such things, and care about knowing such things.

These two sons are also the reason that I have a TV with a picture that is bigger than 19 inches, much bigger than 19 inches. Their logic is that if I am going to review television shows and DVDs, then I ought to be able to see them in full glory. Of course, they didn't pay for the new TV. They just insisted that I get it.

The new TV came into the house about a year ago. Now, they have decided I have to have "surround sound." I can hardly hear the TV set now. What in the world am I supposed to do with surround sound? Still, it is hard to turn down a birthday present and this is what they and their mother gave to me.

The one restriction my wife insisted upon was that no wires were to show when the speakers were installed. This cut out my two boys from installing the equipment. They let wires fall where they may. No, this required a professional.

The "professional" arrived at my house one morning around ten o'clock. He brought an "assistant professional" with him. They went up in my attic and they went under my house. They worked for hours. Finally, they had it all installed and lo and behold there was not a wire showing.

As Mr. Pro was demonstrating how to operate all this sound equipment plus a new DVD player my family had thrown in, he mentioned that it would take two remotes to make it work. For some bizarre reason, I insisted on having an all-in-one remote. He had one available. It cost as much as the gross national product of a small country. Still, I had to be able to receive all this perfect sound and it had to be simple enough for me to get it done, so I purchased it.

Now, I can sit in my office and watch TV shows and DVDs and have the full glory of their sound surrounding me. It comes from the sides, it comes from the back, it comes from all around me.

I have learned a lesson from this sound spectacular. A bad TV show is still a bad TV show. A bad DVD is still a bad DVD. If a program or movie is bad, then it is going to stay bad and all the fancy sound in the world isn't going to help it. You just have the badness enhanced and made clearer.

But a good TV show or DVD, well, it is made better. Those sounds that encompass you are just like sitting in the middle of the action. I may not have thought sound could make a difference but I am now a convert. You hear that!

Wedding Etiquette

Recently, I went to a wedding. Nothing special there as I have been to more than my share during my lifetime. They are always glorious occasions where the bride is radiant and the groom is grinning. They are a tradition in America that time and tide can not erase. But this wedding was different. It was different because of divorce.

The radiant bride and the grinning groom were both from families where the parents were divorced. And the divorced parties had all remarried others. So instead of two families being combined you had four. Now, if you don't think that complicates things, well, you aren't with the program.

First off, there's the question of the best man. Does the groom select his father to stand beside him, or the stepfather who has been there for him? In this case it was the stepfather who was selected. This was as it should be as the father of the groom had been absent from his life for the most part.

Still, the groom wanted his father there so he and his wife as well as the mother shared the parents' row on the groom's side. Across the aisle it was the same. The divorced parties and their new spouses were lined up in one row. The weather was warm, but there was a chill in the air.

We were friends of the groom and when we arrived everyone was outside waiting to be seated. I spoke first to the groom's mother and then went over and spoke to his father. As we all stood around, something funny happened. Remember that scene in *West Side Story* where Tony and Maria meet at the school dance for the very first time? Everyone becomes a blur except for the two of them and they are in clear focus.

I looked at Theresa and John, the parents of the groom. They hadn't been in each other's company in ten years or more. Suddenly, here they were at the wedding of their son. Everyone around them seemed to blur as they turned towards each other.

"I can't believe this day is here," John said.

"It's been a long time coming," answered Theresa.

For just a moment, there was no bitterness, no estrangement, no loss of communication between the two of them. They looked at each other and just for a second they were sharing thoughts about their much-loved son. And then with a blink of an eye the moment was gone, and the world came rushing back.

At the reception John, Jr., made a toast. He raised his glass and said, "There are four families here tonight, together for the first time ever. I want you to know that I love you all. For tonight, we are all family!"

Divorce is a common affliction of today's society. In some cases, it makes a home life situation better. In others, it makes it worse. But in all cases, it is usually the kids who suffer the most.

Luckily, in my friend's life, the families came together to help create a union of two people who were loved by them all. With God's help, they will all be family for a long time to come.

The American Way

A few weeks ago, I spent my weekend at the Mossy Creek Arts and Crafts Fair. As a general rule, something of this nature would not be my thing, but I had been offered a chance to sell copies of my book(s), so to the fair I did go.

Jackie White, who wrote *Whisper to the Black Candle* and *The Empty Nursery* (both true crime books), was my partner in this venture. She and I took our books, set up our tent, and proceeded to watch the world go by while occasionally selling a book or two.

Mossy Creek is set up in some pine woods. The light filters down through the branches of the trees and patterns of light play with the dust and pollen in the air. The ground has been covered with hay and that helps keep down the dust from the dirt.

From where we were seated, I could watch the whole parade of people as they came to the fair. They started arriving around nine in the morning when the air was still chilled and the sky was still cloudy. They came wearing jackets, jeans, and long-sleeved shirts. They came as sisters out on an excursion away from home, or as couples wandering about the area hand in hand.

Some came as families with dad pulling the youngest child in a wagon. In some cases, there were twins in the wagons, who waved as they passed my stand. In every instance, there were smiles on their faces and a friendly wave to be had. No one seemed to be in a hurry and no one seemed to be in a bad mood.

The vendors were mostly selling homemade items. I could watch a man across from us as he carved animals out of wood with a hatchet. He was unbelievably skilled as he molded them with sharp chips that cut through the solid wood. I did notice, however, that quite a few of his fingers were covered with Band-Aids.

Next to us was a lady who made stuffed animals. Now how she did this was a secret I never learned. She insisted though that she created them all and I believed her. She had dragons, hippos, elephants, and dogs. Children rushed to her booth and begged to take one of them home.

On the other side was a man who carved popguns. They made a loud pop when shot and kids loved them too. I wish I had sold as many books as he did guns. They seemed to be one of the most popular items of the weekend.

Food was also on sale. You could get homemade ice cream, a chicken plate with vegetables, barbeque, folded pies, and curly fries. Whoever knew that curly fries, greasy as the day is long, could be so good? And then there was the corn on the cob. People walked around the fair eating corn on the cob like it was cotton candy.

For two days, I watched this panorama of people going around the grounds. They walked, they talked, they shopped, and they greeted one another. They were a friendly bunch and some even knew a few of the vendors by name. This confused me until I learned that some of the vendors have been coming to Mossy Creek for years.

Mossy Creek is a Middle Georgia event, but from what I learned in talking with the people who attend twice a year, fairs of this type take place all over the country. It isn't just a Georgia thing; it isn't just a Southern thing. This tradition of shopping for handmade goods is nationwide.

For some reason this pleases me. I like to think that all across America people are buying hand-carved ducks, stuffed cocker spaniels, and ears of corn. It is one of the last traditions left for the entire family to enjoy. It gets them away from the TV set and out of the house, back to a world where people are polite and friendly. It is pure Americana through and through and I loved it!

Biloxi Happiness

Biloxi is the Las Vegas east of the Mississippi River. Those who don't want to drive or fly for a long distance can just head the car down the highway and hit Biloxi in just a few hours. At least, someone like me who lives in Georgia can. And recently I did.

A friend and I took a three-day, two-night jaunt to this city by the sea. We left our homes at four-thirty in the morning and were in the casinos of Biloxi by nine their time. The first order of business was to eat. The casinos have some great buffets and we gorged out on the breakfast buffet.

I ate so much that I didn't need to eat again until the next morning. Honest, I didn't. Of course, you get free drinks constantly so that helped keep the stomachs full. Let me correct that statement. The drinks aren't really free.

The first time I went I thought they were. I just kept ordering different things and when they arrived I would smile and say thank you. But it got harder and harder to find a waitress to take my order. Someone clued me in and told me you are supposed to tip, then the waiters/waitresses magically appeared again.

The new thing in the casinos is to have pay-offs done with slips of paper. No longer do you have nickels, quarters or dollars flowing out with a ching, ching, ching. You just get a slip of paper saying you are entitled to a certain amount of money. This keeps your hands clean, makes you gamble faster, and cuts down on noise pollution.

I miss the coins and I miss the ching, ching, ching. It doesn't seem as much like the old slot machines without the handles to pull and the coins to fall. But all things have to end and the day of the coin has come and gone.

It is really interesting to watch someone play the slots. If they hit a big jackpot, they will yell and scream and ask people to come look. There are no strangers on the slot machine circuit. Winners know and love everyone.

For those losers, it's a different story. Losers don't want anyone looking at them. And when they finally lose all the money they have, or have allotted, they sneak furtively away from the machine, looking neither right nor left.

When I go to Biloxi, I take a specified amount of money and spend no more, no less. When it is gone, it is gone. There is no going to the ATM machine, no putting cash advances on credit cards. I treat the slots as a game of fun not a chance for retirement.

When I am sitting at the slot machines, my mind tunes out on any problems I have or any obligations that are upcoming. I am in the zone and am feeling no stress, depression, or anguish. It is like I am in suspended animation.

Yep, I love Biloxi. I only get there a few times a year but when I do it is fun time from start to finish. Neil Simon wrote about "Biloxi Blues." In my opinion there is only "Biloxi happiness."

Daddy's Hands

When I was around twelve years old, it dawned on me that my father was old. At least it seemed to me that he was old. He was in his forties at the time but to my mind he had one foot in the grave.

My friend Agnes and I discussed this one night sitting on the curb at the corner of Holland Street and Stonewall Avenue. Agnes and I were prone to have these deep philosophical discussions from time to time.

The topic on this particular night was age and how we didn't want to ever get old. I remember asking Agnes what she thought it would be like to be Daddy's age, and whether or not when you reached that age all you thought about was dying. We both agreed that being young was far superior to anything age could offer.

At that time, it really did seem we were living in the golden age of life. We were children of middle-class families who gave us basically everything we wanted. Or maybe it was that we just didn't really want that much. We were young, healthy, and happy and living in the South. The world was our oyster and we knew we had it made.

Daddy on the other hand was old, hard working, and had lots of responsibilities. He was a bread salesman who got up at four every morning and started his day. In winter, he had to venture out into the cold and in summer he had to cope with the heat. Nope, I knew I had it better than he did.

A few days later on a Sunday, we went to church. I was sitting next to Daddy and while the preacher preached I was studying his hands. There were a variety of nicks and cuts on them as well as calluses and wrinkles. I felt the roughness of them and knew that they were the hands of an old man.

Last Sunday, I was in church and as the preacher preached I studied my hands. They are wrinkled and rough, and there are even a few age spots beginning to show. Or maybe those are just freckles I had never noticed before. They aren't as callused as my father's hands were, but then he always did do more manual labor than I.

Still, they are more my father's hands than they are mine. He has been dead for five years now, but his hands are still with me. My wife says the same thing about her hands. She says they look just like her mother's.

But now that I am older, I realize that being my age is the reward of my life. I wouldn't want to be twelve or sixteen or even twenty-one again. I am one of the fortunate ones who is older, healthier, independent, and happy. I can do what I please with no one to boss me around, and I have a little bit of money to do it with. Life is good.

My Daddy had some good years before he died also. He lived to reach retirement age and had the joy of being financially independent and able to do some of the things he enjoyed. He was able to see his grandchildren born and could hold them and play with them. They learned to love him and his hands as much as I did.

Kids think they have the world by a string, but really they don't. In many cases, the poem that says, "grow old along with me, / the best is yet to be" is the absolute truth. If we are lucky life gets better and better. I hope it is that way for you.

Fly-by Life

The older I get the more I understand about life. Whereas, when I was young I thought life was centuries long, I now see that it all goes by in the blink of an eye. I have almost gotten hedonistic in my thinking since I realize there is nothing gained by working hard, unless you like the act of working hard. Amassing a fortune is fine for those who follow you, but by the time you get around to getting rich your time is going to be almost up.

So, why not just do those things in life that you enjoy? That doesn't mean you shouldn't support yourself and not be a burden on society, I am not that extreme. But you should find the job that suits your talents and your enthusiasm and go for it.

I spent too many years practicing law when I didn't want to be a lawyer. Therefore, I was adamant that my boys would go into careers they enjoyed. I remember telling each of them if he decided on the last day of his final year in college that he had picked the wrong major, let me know. I would find some way to support his new career choice.

Of course, I was lucky; both of my sons knew from an early age what they wanted to do with their lives. My oldest started writing about sports when he was fourteen. He was sports editor of the local paper when he was sixteen. Now he is an editor with *Baseball America* and is happy as can be.

My youngest started working in a church as a youth activities director when a sophomore in college. Now he is youth minister at the First Methodist Church of Moultrie, Georgia. He loves what he does and he is good at it.

And me, well, I don't practice law any more. I review movies on television for the local NBC affiliate and write reviews and other entertainment articles for newspapers and online websites. I, too, am a very happy man, and most of that happiness just comes from understanding life.

But I don't understand death. I don't understand the logic by which it takes some of us quickly and leaves others alone for years. This death thing is on my mind because a friend of mine lost a child recently. He and his wife put the baby down one night and when they went to wake him up the next morning he was dead.

The child was fifteen months old and so far the doctors can find no explanation for why he died. He just did. As you can expect, the entire family is devastated, and I am full of shock and sorrow for my friend.

The main question they and I have is, Why? Why did this happen? Why didn't it happen to someone else? What could have been done to prevent it? And there are no answers for any of those questions.

I am a person of faith, and someday I think I will get answers to those kinds of questions. In the meantime, I am going to enjoy my family, my friends, and my life in general. If it is going to fly by, as it is doing, I am going to thoroughly enjoy the ride.

The Other Fork

Do you ever think what your life might have been if you had taken that other fork in the road? Would you still be the person you are today, or would your life have taken you into an entirely different direction? Of course, we will never know, but it does sometimes pique my brain to wonder about it.

My father was a bread salesman until he retired. He was able to provide for his family, but he never made a lot of money. He would often say that he wondered what would have happened if he had taken his brother-in-law's offer of a job in Ohio. That was back a few years after he and my mother married. Uncle Jack was a foreman at one of the steel mills in Ohio and offered my Dad a job if he would move the family there.

The Coopers were a big family and all the brothers lived in Clinton. My Dad's two sisters had married and moved away, but the boys all stayed in the area. My father couldn't stand the thought of being away from all of his kin, so he opted to stay where he was. So my brother and I didn't grow up as Northerners but were Southern through and through.

My life was determined by a TV show. I was inspired to be a lawyer by watching *Perry Mason* and as a result went to law school. Now, what if I had been inspired by *Medical Center* and had decided to be a doctor? Who knows where that would have taken me?

Also, my brother and sister-in-law arranged a blind date for me with my future wife. They had never set me up before and I really hadn't asked that they do it this time. They thought it might be a good way to get me to visit them in St. Petersburg, Florida, so they called and said they had someone they wanted me to meet. Why I agreed, I will never know. Maybe that is what they call fate or kismet.

From that one date my future wife and I began to date steadily. I drove from Warner Robins, Georgia, where I was stationed in the Air Force, to St. Petersburg every other weekend. That was our dating pattern. After a year and a half, we married.

While still stationed at Robins Air Force Base I picked up the base newspaper. There were listings for the movies that were playing on base or were coming soon. The base movies were generally a few weeks behind the local theaters, so I had seen all the movies. That night I sat down and wrote short reviews of all of them and mailed them in to the editor without signing my name.

A few days later they were printed. I called up the editor and told him he had run my reviews. He was glad to know who had sent them and asked if I wanted to keep doing them. I agreed and that is how I began my writing career.

Life is a combination of our choices, be they big or small. I could easily have been a doctor living in Ohio who married a local girl and stayed there forever. Instead, I have the life I have and it is a good one. I am one of those amazingly fortunate people who wouldn't change a thing.

There are still choices ahead and forked roads. I just pray my luck continues and I make the right decisions. We never know what the future holds. We can always look back and remember, but we can't look ahead and forecast the future.

Hello, Grinchy

Christmas has not arrived yet and the "Grinch" in me is already in control. It started a few days before Thanksgiving. I could feel my usually cheerful self beginning to fade. The smile became forced; the cheer became fake. All I wanted to do was escape to my bedroom and burrow my head under the covers. All I wanted to do was shout, "I don't like holidays! I have never liked holidays!"

I am a person who likes order. I like the sameness of things. My favorite days of the week are Monday through Friday. On Saturdays and Sundays order does not reign. It is chaos time. You do one thing one weekend and another thing the next.

Basically, my days follow a format. I get up around seven-thirty. I sit down at my computer and go through various errands such as checking my stock listings, personal webpage, top movie list, Drudge Report, etc.

Then I call my bank and check off the checks that have cleared. Don't ask me why, but I enjoy doing this. Again, it is an order thing. I also make a list every day of things I need to do and as I do them I check them off. This gives me a sense of accomplishment and achievement.

Around ten o'clock, I go to my favorite convenience store and get a soft drink and a pack of peanut butter and cheese crackers. I also get a copy of *USA Today*, which I read while sitting in my car, drinking my drink and eating my crackers. When I get home, I work the crossword puzzle in the paper. I do it with a ballpoint pen so I can't make erasures.

During the morning I also watch some television programs I have to review, or read a book I am reviewing. At lunchtime I generally go to Wendy's and have a Biggie chili, a Biggie fry, and a Biggie diet coke. I also ask for a big senior discount (a little senior citizen humor there).

In the afternoon, I go to a local movie theater and see a new movie. When it is over and I get home, it is time for my wife to arrive home from her job. We discuss her day and then I do some more writing. We go out to eat and then come home and I write some more.

That is a typical day. It is not the most exciting way to live, but it is orderly and consistent. It also is broken up periodically by my need to do some interviews, go to Atlanta for a movie screening, or visits from my children and grandchildren.

The point is that I know basically what to expect from the time I wake up to the time I go to bed—and that sameness gives me security and enjoyment. When a holiday comes along that is all messed up.

That is when the Grinch rears his ugly head and I have to become some kind of mechanical man who gets through these days as best as possible. I do my best to be cheerful and to make all the right noises and responses, but my family and my closest friends can see right through me.

The question is why am I that way? And why are there others in this world who are also this way? I haven't heard it defined, but it is something like the "anti-holiday syndrome." I know there are tons of you out there who feel the same way I do. To you I say, just know you have someone who understands the way you feel.

Happy non-holidays!

Dance, Genna, Dance

It is different when you have a girl in the family. Much different. You suddenly are subjected to tea parties and baby-doll events. One day, you are working towards retirement and the next you are going to dance recitals. At least, that is what happened to my life when Genna came along.

I always wanted a daughter. Don't take that to mean I don't love my sons. I do. I have loved them totally from the day they were born. Still, I always thought we might have one more child and that it would be a girl. If you haven't learned by now that things don't always happen the way you think they will, well, learn it quickly because that is oh-so true.

Anyway, I had to wait to have grandchildren before I got the girl in the family. She came; she saw; she conquered. She arrived like a whirlwind and she has kept us spinning ever since. She knows what is best for us, for her parents, and especially for her younger brother. Is she bossy? A little. Is she wonderful? A lot.

This past weekend, she had her first dance recital. It was on Saturday and prior to the recital she was going to a Santa Claus breakfast. It started at eight in the morning. My wife and I live ninety-plus miles from Genna, so if we were going to make it to the breakfast we had to leave our house by six in the morning, meaning we had to get up at five in the morning.

Generally, I don't get up at five. I could actually count the times I have gotten up that early on one hand. But Genna was going to be disappointed if we weren't there, and we don't disappoint Genna. We got up at five and were there before eight.

I noticed as we were driving into Moultrie (where my son and his family live) that the temperature was in the low 30s. I remarked to my wife that it didn't seem that cold. Of course it didn't seem that cold. I was driving around in a heated car.

At ten-thirty that morning when we went to the courthouse lawn where the dance recital was being held, it was still in the 30s or maybe in the low 40s. There was also a vicious wind blowing. Why they would have a dance recital outside is beyond me, but it is tradition in Moultrie to do it this way.

I have never been so cold in my life. We sat on cement steps to watch this event and my rear end almost froze off. It was painfully cold. Still, when Genna came out with her group to do the Teddy Bear dance, the sun broke through and warmed my body and my soul.

It was one-two kick, one-two kick, hold up the Teddy Bear, and turn around. Then they did it over a few more times. I swear my granddaughter looked like Ginger Rogers doing that routine. She definitely has talent. And true grit. Anyone who could dance in that cold has my admiration and those three- and four-year-olds did it to perfection.

I don't remember doing anything like that with my boys until they were in high school and playing football. Then we did suffer through some cold Friday nights. But with girls it is different. They start early and drag you kicking and screaming into their world. At least Genna does. She is the little girl I always wanted and I will follow her anywhere.

That Mysterious Connection

Much has been written about the dynamics between fathers and daughters, as well as mothers and sons. There is also a mysterious connection between fathers and sons. The father sees in his son his disappearing youth, and sons see in their fathers the men they hope to be. The bond is usually a strong one or a loose one with no in between.

My father constantly let me know he loved me. Up till the day he died, he never passed up an opportunity to tell me. Still, when he died, I knew everything about him that most people knew and nothing more. He was an open book to his family and friends, but I wanted to know what went on between the lines. Either he didn't know or was reluctant to share it. In either case, he was and will always remain a mystery.

When I was a little boy, Daddy was a great playmate. He would wrestle with my brother and me or take us to the playground to play. He was an easy touch and would give me just about anything I asked for, whether I needed it or not. Luckily for him, I asked for very little.

My mother died just as I was entering my teenage years. This meant my father was the only one I could turn to for all of my numerous problems, and I had tons, both real and imaginary. The biggest problem though was that my father did not want to deal with my problems. I remember going to him with a list of obstacles I felt were in my life. His response was, "Don't tell me those things, they give me a headache."

What you have to understand is that my father had an abnormally high threshold of pain and never, ever got headaches.

I had heard that all my life, so I instantly knew he just didn't want to be bothered. As I have grown older, I realize it wasn't that he didn't care, he just didn't know how to handle the problems of a teenage son.

That established the pattern of our life. In this respect, he became the child and I became the parent. I listened to his problems, but I never told him mine. And though he told me his problems, usually of the financial kind, he never let down his guard to let me see the real person underneath the cheerful exterior.

With my sons, I have tried to be real. I am not an advocate of parents being buddies with their kids while they are growing up, but now that they are grown I want them to enjoy me as a person. To reach this goal, I talk with them adult to adult. They know my likes, dislikes, and even my quirks. I enjoy talking with them and I hope they enjoy talking with me.

My conversations with my father were all superficial. I never tried to talk deeply with him and he never revealed any depth to me. Our talks might as well have been all about the weather. We never argued; we never debated; we never did anything but swap pleasantries.

My father never let an opportunity pass to tell me he loved me. I just wish he had loved me enough to let me see the real person he was. Maybe he was afraid to show the man behind the mask, or maybe there just wasn't anyone back there.

Down Memory Lane

Last week I was in St. Petersburg, Florida, visiting my in-laws. My wife and her mother went out to do some shopping, so my father-in-law and I sat down to watch some TV. While flipping through the channels, we came across *White Christmas*.

Now, don't say you haven't watched it. Everyone has watched it at least once or twice or a million times. It's just one of those movies that has become a tradition, just like *It's a Wonderful Life* or *Miracle on 34th Street*. Plus, who can resist hearing Bing Crosby and Rosemary Clooney sing songs such as "White Christmas" and "Count Your Blessings"?

Anyway, while we were watching, my father-in-law began to reminisce about his World War II days, and especially the time he spent at the Stage Door Canteen in Hollywood. This was the first time I had ever heard him talk about this and I was immediately interested.

He mentioned that when he and some of the other guys were at the Stage Door Canteen that they asked Bing Crosby for his autograph and he said no. "He just wasn't a real friendly guy," said Joe, my father-in-law. "Real stand-offish."

"The guy who was really friendly was William Bendix," Joe continued. "He was in that TV series *The Life of Riley* and he was real funny and told a lot of funny stories. He seemed glad to be meeting us all and didn't seem to be bothered by us wanting autographs."

Joe went on to tell me about all the big stars who were at the Canteen and how they would dance with them or just make conversation. "Do you know who the best dancer was?" he asked.

I immediately thought of Ginger Rogers, Ann Miller, and other known dancers of that era. But Joe shook his head whenever I mentioned one of these names.

"Bette Davis," he said. "She was the best. She was like dancing with Jello, the way she would just glide around the room. And she liked to dance. You could tell it."

As I listened to Joe talk about these days fifty years or more ago, I realized that the people who knew these stars and saw those movies originally would soon be gone. The forties were known as the "golden age of Hollywood" and the stars of that time were names that were bigger than life.

There are a couple of generations now that don't know who William Holden was, or even Grace Kelly. Some of them are so young that if you mention TV's Carson they think of Carson Daly instead of Johnny Carson. It's a new day, a new age, and a new group of celebrities.

Still, every once in a while it is fun to look back instead of ahead. And it is good to talk to someone of the age that they knew about those stars personally. Each generation has its heroes and icons and to the men and women of the World War II era there were none as bright as Bing Crosby and Bette Davis. They are gone, but in the hearts and minds of an older generation they are still the top stars.

Catching up with the Kershaws

A few days ago I was sitting at my desk writing a movie review when the phone rang. I answered and a woman's voice said she was looking for Jackie Cooper. I said that was me, and she replied, "I think you are my cousin."

I asked her name and she said it was Priscilla, and I knew immediately that she was right. She is my cousin, my first cousin. Her father Jerry Kershaw and my mother Virginia were brother and sister. He and his family lived in Gadsden, Alabama, where my mother had been raised, while we had become a South Carolina family.

Every year when we would go to visit my grandparents, we would always see Uncle Jerry and his family. There were two daughters. The older one, Priscilla, was my brother's age, and the younger one, Sue, was my age. Sue was also the favorite of my grandfather and we were all jealous of her.

After my mother died when I was fourteen, we lost contact with most of the Kershaw family. There had been nine children in the family, four boys and five girls, and my mother was the youngest girl and Uncle Jerry was the youngest boy. With that many aunts and uncles there had to be a lot of cousins out there.

Finding as many of these cousins as possible had become Priscilla's mission and she had accomplished a lot before she found me. She named off one cousin after another with whom she had talked. Some of them had names I recognized while others did not.

One particular branch of the family was all gone. I asked about Velma, Carl, Mickey, and Sylvia and she responded that they were all dead. I was staggered. One whole family—my mother's sister, her husband, and their two children were all deceased. And there were many more that were gone. In the course of a two-hour phone conversation, I learned that many of the people I had known as a young boy were no longer alive.

What was even more amazing was talking with Priscilla about my grandparents. I had never known that much about them, but Priscilla knew tons. The first thing she mentioned was that my grandfather Kershaw was from Lynchburg, Virginia. I had always thought he was born and raised in Gadsden, Alabama, because that is where he raised his family. Nope, he was a Virginian. Perhaps that is why my mother was named Virginia. Who knows?

Then she mentioned that my grandfather had been married to another woman prior to marrying my grandmother. Now, that was a shock. I grew up thinking no one in my family had ever gotten divorced. My poor old divorced brother was almost drummed out of the family when he ended his marriage. And here Granddaddy Kershaw had been divorced way back when nobody got divorced.

By the time Priscilla and I ended our conversation, we had bonded again. The years between talks may have been many but the bond of family ties still existed. It's strange how that is. You think you have forgotten all about some people, but a phone call is all it takes to renew the relationship. And now we have e-mail to help us keep in touch.

So if you have someone in your family with whom you haven't talked in a decade or so, go to the Internet and get busy. In this age, you can find anyone. Family is so important and so is family history. We all need to know who we are and what our background is. It has been said, "The roots of the present lie deep in the past." Our families are the ones who give us our roots.

Epilogue

The sun is setting now taking my memories once more to sleep. Tomorrow, it will rise again and a new crop of memories will be made. Some will be good and some not so good, but all of them will be mine, as all of your will be yours.

It is important for you to share your memories. You can do this by telling them to others, writing them down, or getting them on tape. They are your history and your legacy. They will live long after you are gone. The people who come after you will want these shared memories so they can better know who you were and what you were.

As the day ends, my memories flicker through my mind like fireflies. Word by word I capture them and press them to these pages. Here they will live for eternity.

The road stretches out before me with sunrises left to come. I am still a part of the journey, still a part of this grand adventure we call life. I hope you have enjoyed this walk we had for the time of these pages. Come walk with me again.

Jackie K. Cooper
November 1, 2007